Scot land the best

PETER IRVINE

exclusive edition for
SCOTLAND*on*SUNDAY

Author and journalist Pete Irvine is also Scotland's leading-edge event organizer. His company, Unique Events, created Edinburgh's annual Hogmanay Programme twelve years ago in the year that he started this book; it has become the world's biggest New Year's celebration. He is also the director of Scotland's annual contemporary-art gatherings – the Glasgow Art Fair and Glasgow International – and of the annual festival that celebrates the life and spirit of Robert Burns, Burns and a' That.

In 2000 he received the Silver Thistle Award for his 'outstanding contribution to the development of tourism in Scotland' and the MBE for services to Edinburgh.

HarperCollins Publishers
Westerhill Road, Bishopbriggs, Glasgow G64 2QT

The Collins website is www.collins.co.uk

This edition has been produced exclusively for *Scotland on Sunday*

© Peter Irvine 2006

ISBN 0 00 773557-X

Printed and bound in Great Britain by
Clays Ltd, St Ives plc

Contents

Twelve years ago when I started doing *Scotland the Best* it was a journey of discovery for me. I didn't know Scotland that well, either! It took over two years and the book emerged as I went along. Since then, and knowing Scotland a good deal better, I've been able to rely on researchers although I've always done the bulk of it myself. However, for the 2006/07 edition I decided to go back to basics and as much as possible to visit everywhere again – myself. I wanted to restore the high standard that I'd looked for originally.

I've always seen it as my task to find the best places and my duty to bring them to your attention. It's my view that Scotland is doing better than ever and although I've tried to be more rigorous in the new edition, and to raise the bar (culling to be kind; perhaps losing friends in the process), there's certainly no shortage of places replacing those that have been lost.

Space – or the lack of it – dictates that while this little edition gives a flavour of the book, much has had to be omitted. This doesn't just mean entries themselves: ways of navigating the pages as you travel the country – notably by maps and by cross-references, which can tell you, for example, about a good pub in the area while you're out on your walk – haven't crossed over from the main book.

While everything in *Scotland the Best* is notable, some places even in this vaunted company are better than others. In my scheme of things these are awarded an additional 'tick'. If a place is among the very best of its type in the UK (and this includes landscape features as well as places to visit and to sleep or eat), it's awarded two ticks. Three ticks are reserved for those places that are among the best in the world or simply unique.

I may have been less generous with the ticks in this edition, but it's all in the cause of raising the standard. The further afield and the more often we travel, the more we see that we will have to strive if Scotland is to be the best small county in the world. But it will be worth it.

Don't go as quickly as I did. Happy trails.

Pete Irvine
Edinburgh, January 2006

The Ticks

All places listed here are notable in some way; those which are outstanding have been 'awarded' a tick.

 Amongst the very best in Scotland

Amongst the best (of its type) in the UK

Amongst the best (of its type) in the world, or simply unique

Listings generally are not in an order of merit although if there is one outstanding item it will always be at the top of the page and this obviously includes anything which has been given a tick.

The Hotel Codes

Under each hotel recommended is a band of codes as follows:

20RMS JAN-DEC T/T PETS CC KIDS LOTS

20RMS means the hotel has 20 bedrooms in total.

JAN-DEC means the hotel is open all year round. **APR-OCT** means approximately from the beginning of April to the end of October.

T/T refers to the facilities: **T/** means there are direct-dial phones in the bedrooms while **/T** means there are TVs in the bedrooms.

PETS means the hotel accepts dogs and other pets, probably under certain conditions. It's usually best to check first.

XPETS indicates that the hotel does not generally accept pets.

CC means the hotel accepts major credit cards (e.g. Mastercard, Visa).

XCC means the hotel does not accept credit cards.

KIDS means children are welcome; there may be special provisions.

XKIDS does not necessarily mean that children are not welcome, only that special provisions/rates are not usually made. Check by phone.

LOTS Rooms which cost more than £80 per person per night.

EXP Expensive: £58-80. **MED.EX** Medium (expensive): £42-58.

MED.INX Medium (inexpensive): £35-42.

INX Inexpensive: £28-35. **CHP** Cheap: less than £28.

Rates are per person per night and should be used only to give an impression of cost. They are based on 2005 prices.

The Restaurant Codes

Found under the name and address of all restaurant entries. It refers to the price of an average dinner per person with a starter, a main course and dessert. It doesn't include wine, coffee or extras.

EXP Expensive: more than £32. **MED** Medium: £22-32.

INX Inexpensive: £14-22. **CHP** Cheap: under £14.

LO means last orders at the kitchen.

10pm/10.30pm means usually 10pm Mon-Fri, 10.30pm at w/ends.

The Walk Codes

Found under the name of each walk. **2-10km CIRC BIKE 1-A-1**

2-10km means the walk(s) may vary in length from 2km to 10km.

CIRC means the walk can be circular; **xCIRC** is not.

BIKE indicates a path suitable for ordinary bikes; **xBIKE** means unsuitable for cycling; **mtBIKE** means suitable for mountain bikes.

The **1-A-1** Code:

The first number shows how easy the walk is (**1**: easy; **2** medium difficulty, e.g. standard hillwalking; **3** difficult: preparation & map needed).

The letters (**A, B or C**) show how easy it is to find the path (**A**: easy; **B**: not obvious, but you'll get there; **C**: map & preparation/guide needed).

The last number (**1, 2 or 3**) shows required footwear (**1** ordinary shoes, incl trainers, probably okay unless the ground is very wet; **2**: walking boots needed; **3** serious walking/hiking boots needed).

Other Abbreviations:

Aber	Aberdeen	L	loch
accom	accommodation	LA	last admission
adj	adjacent	min(s)	minute(s)
admn	admission	mt(s)	mountain(s)
app	approach	N	north
approx	approximately	nr	near
atmos	atmosphere	o/look	overlook(s)/ing
AYR	all year round	pl	place
		pt	point/port
bedrms	bedrooms	R	river
betw	between	rep	reputation
br	bridge	refurb	refurbished/ment
BYOB	bring your own bottle	restau	restaurant
		rm(s)	room(s)
C	century	rt	right
cl	closes/closed	S	south
cotts	cottages	☕	worth visiting for the tearoom alone
E	east	tho	though
Edin	Edinburgh	thro	through
esp	especially	TIC	Tourist Information Centre
excl	excluding/excellent		
exp	expensive	t/off	turn off
facs	facilities	v	very
ft	fort	VC	visitor centre
gdn(s)	garden(s)	vegn	vegetarian
Glas	Glasgow	W	west
gr	great	w/end(s)	weekend(s)
hr(s)	hour(s)		
incl	including		
inexp	inexpensive		
jnct	junction		

Part 1

Scotland the best

Wha's Like Us?

Wemyss Bay-Rothesay Ferry

01475 650100
Calmac

Wemyss Bay's glass-roofed station (60km from Glas on the A78) is redolent of an age-old terminus; the frequent ferry has all the Scottish traits and sausage rolls you can handle; and Rothesay with its period mansions appears like a gentle watercolour from holidays past. Visit its Victorian toilet and Mount Stuart. Both are superb.

Loch Etive Cruises

01866 822430,
though booking
not essential.
Easter-mid Oct.
Leaves 12-2pm
(not Sat).

From Taynuilt (Oban 20km) thro the narrow waters of atmospheric L Etive for 3hrs in a small cruiser with indoor and outdoor seating. Pier is 2km from Taynuilt crossroads on A85. Also **Loch Shiel Cruises**: 01687 470322. From nr Glenfinnan House Hotel on the Road to the Isles, the A830, Various trips on glorious L Shiel.

Glenelg-Kylerhea

01599 511302
Apr-Oct
(frequent)
9am-5.45pm &
Sun in summer
(from 10am).

The shorter of the 2 ferry trips to Skye, and the best way to get there if you're not pushed for time. The drive to Glenelg from the A87 is spectacular and so is this 5min crossing of the deep Narrows of Kylerhea. Otter-watch hide at Kylerhea.

Corran Ferry

01855 841243
Contin till
8.50pm summer,
7.50pm winter.
Later w/ends.

From Ardgour on A861-Nether Lochaber on the A82 across the narrows of L Linnhe. A convenient 5min crossing to points S of Mallaig takes you to the wildernesses of Moidart and Ardnamurchan. A charming, fondly regarded journey in its own right.

Maid of the Forth Cruise to Inchcolm Is.

0131 331 4857
1hr 30mins
ashore. Mar-Oct.

The wee boat (though they say it holds 225 people) leaves daily at different times (phone for details) from Hawes Pier in S

Queensferry (15km Central Edin via A90) opposite the Hawes Inn, just under the famous br & from Newhaven Harbour in town. 45min trips under the br and on to pretty Inchcolm Island with walks, an impressive ruined abbey, birdlife and seals.

The Waverley

0845 130 4647

'The World's Last Sea-going Paddle Steamer' which plied the Clyde in the glorious 'Doon the Water' days is *the* way to see the W Coast. Sailings from Glas Anderson Quay (and some days Greenock or Ayr) to Rothesay, Kyles of Bute, Arran.

The West Highland Line

*Rail info:
08457 484950
Trains for Mallaig
leave Glas Queen
St 3 times a day
and take about
5hrs.*

One of Europe's most picturesque rail journeys and the best way to get to Skye from the S. Travel to Ft William from Glas then relax and watch the stunning scenery and Bonnie Prince Charlie country go by. Viaducts (incl the Harry Potter one) and tunnels over loch and down dale.

From Inverness

*Info on
08457 484950
Inverness-Kyle of
Lochalsh:
2hrs 30 mins.
3 trains a day.
Inverness-Wick:
3hrs 50 mins.
3 trains a day in
summer.*

Two mesmerising rail journeys start from Inverness. For the Kyle of Lochalsh trip, get a window seat and take an atlas: the last section through Glen Carron and around the coast at L Carron is especially fine. Inverness-Wick takes 3hr 50min. The section skirting the E coast from Lairg-Helmsdale is full of drama, followed by the transfixing monotony of the Flow Country.

The Plane to Barra

*0870 8509850
12-seater Otter
leaves and lands
daily according to
the tide.*

BA's Glas-Barra flight is special not just for the other islands it passes over, but because Barra's airport is on Cockleshell Beach in the N of the island (11 km from Castlebay) after a splendid app.

What Scots Gave The World

The population of Scotland has never been much over 5 million and yet we discovered, invented or manufactured for the first time the following quite important things.

The decimal point	Interferon
The hypodermic syringe	The photocopier
Logarithms	The pneumatic tyre
Finger-printing	Video
The Bank of England	The pedal bicycle
The kaleidoscope	The telephone
The overdraft	The modern road surface
Anaesthesia	Television
Cannabis (the active principle)	Geology
Antiseptics	Radar
Documentary films	Artificial ice
Golf clubs	Helium
Colour photographs	Morphine
The 18-hole golf course	Neon
Encyclopaedia Britannica	Ante-natal clinics
Tennis courts	The telegraph
Postcards	Bovril
The bowling green	Street lighting
The gas mask	Marmalade
Writing paper	The lawnmower
The theory of combustion	The fountain pen
The thermometer	Kinetic energy
The advertising film	The Mackintosh
The gravitating compass	Electric light
The bus	Gardenias
The threshing machine	The alpha chip
The steam engine	Dolly, the cloned sheep
Insulin	The Thermos flask
The locomotive	Obstetric ultrasound
Penicillin	*Auld Lang Syne*
The fax machine	

Part 2

Scotland the best

The Best Places to Stay & Eat

Gleneagles

Auchterarder
01764 662231
271RMS
JANDEC T/T PETS
CC KIDS LOTS

Off A9 and signposted. Scotland's truly luxurious resort hotel. All sport & leisure activities you could want incl shooting, riding, fishing, off-roading (even jeeps for kids), 2 pools with outdoor tub, spa. Oh & world-renowned golf (3 courses). The new wing 'Braid House' contemporary & remote (in the 'handset to control temp, lights, curtains & fireplace' sense). A range of dining options and Andrew Fairlie's intimate dining rm is considered by many to offer the best dining in Scotland. Quintessentially Scottish Gleneagles has airs & graces but it's a friendly old place too.

Glenapp Castle

Nr Ballantrae
01465 831212
17RMS EASTER-
OCT T/T PETS CC
KIDS LOTS AND
LOTS

Home of Inchcape family for most of 20thC, this luxury manor opened as a hotel in first year of 21st. Run by Graham & Fay Cowan. Fabulous restoration of a house that fell into disuse in the 1990s. Excellent and studied service, good food (3 AA rosettes), impeccable environment. Rms are individually beautful; suites are enormous. The price includes just about everything, so relax and join this effortless house party. A southern secret!

Isle Of Eriska

Ledaig
01631 720371
22RMS FEB-DEC
T/T PETS CC
KIDS LOTS

20km N Oban (signed from A85). As you drive over the Victorian iron br you enter a more tranquil, gracious world. Comfortable baronial house with fastidious service. All facs are here if you feel like action, but it's v pleasant just to stay still. Spa suites. Dining, with a Scottish flavour and impeccable local ingredients from a rich backyard and bay, has 3 AA rosettes under chef Robert MacPherson. 5 new rms by the spa incl 3 with own outside hot tubs.

Kinnaird

Dunkeld
01796 482440
9RMS (8 COTT)
JAN-DEC T/T
PETS CC KIDS
LOTS

12km N of Dunkeld via A9 and B898 for Dalguise. A bucolic setting where this country house envelops you with good taste and comfort. There's a teddy on your bed and a stylish 'K' on everything. Gr snooker rm and drawing rm warmed by open fires. Jacket & tie preferred. V fine dining in v fine dining room. 'The Retreat' upstairs does 'treatments'. Silently beyond the grounds, endless traffic ploughs N and S on the A9. One day you'll join it again. Until then, live Kinnaird.

Knockinaam Lodge

Portpatrick
01776 810471
9RMS MAR-DEC
T/T PETS CC KIDS
LOTS

An ideal place to lie low; an historic Victorian house nestled on a cove. The Irish coastline is the only thing on the horizon, apart from discreet service and excellent food (Michelin chef Tony Pierce excels with a fixed menu full of surprises). Winston Churchill was once v comfortable here, too! Superb wine & whisky lists. 15km S of Stranraer, off A77 nr Lochans.

Greywalls

East Lothian
01620 842144
23RMS APR-OCT
T/T PETS CC
XKIDS LOTS

36km E of Edin off A198 just beyond Gullane. Close to Edinburgh & adj the rarified world of Muirfield, but one of the most homely & aesthetically pleasing co-house hotels in the UK. No grey walls here but warm sandstone and light, summery public rms in this Lutyens-designed manor with fabulous gdns attributed to Gertrude Jekyll. The look makes it special and the roses are legendary. Sculpture from Edin's Scottish Gallery occ in summer. Lovely dining rm; indeed all the public rms are homely & full of nice books & things. A brilliant summer house hotel – seems a pity to waste it only on golfers!

Superlative Country-House Hotels

Cromlix House

Dunblane
01786 822125
14RMS(8SUITES)
JAN-DEC T/T
PETS CC KIDS
LOTS

3km from A9 & 4km from town on B8033; foll signs for Perth, then Kinbuck. A leisurely drive thro' old estate with splended mature woodlands to this spacious country mansion both sumptuous & homely. New ownership autumn '05 but no immediate changes planned. 3000 acres of meadows & fishing lochs.

Raemoir House

Banchory
01330 824884
20RMS & SELF-CAT
JAN-DEC T/T
PETS CC KIDS
LOTS

5km N from town via A980. Romantic, quirky mansion with something that sets it apart. Old-fashioned v individual comfy rms given contemporary details. Flowers everywhere, candles at night. 9-hole golf and tennis. Stable annex and self-cat apts. Chef is Grant Walker; dinner a treat & lots of public space to slouch about in. Event prog incl theatre on the lawn. Bliss!

Ballachulish House

Ballachulish
01855 811266
8RMS JAN-DEC
T/X XPETS CC
KIDS EXP/LOTS

On A828 to Oban; not to be confused with the nearby Ballachulish hotel. This small co house hotel has become a W of Scotland destination. Chef Allan Donald goes from strength to strength winning all awards going. Gr b/fast to fuel Glencoe walking. Sometimes piper with dinner. House v Scottish and makes much of its historical background.

Roxburghe Hotel

Nr Kelso
01573 450331
22RMS JAN-DEC
T/T PETS CC
KIDS EXP

The best co-house hotel in the Borders. Rms distinctive, all light with garden views. Reliable wine list and Keith Short's safe hands in the kitchen. The 18-hole championship-standard golf course is challenging in a beautiful riverside setting. 'Health & Beauty Suite' for golf widows. Personal, not overbearing service.

Ardanaiseig

Loch Awe
01866 833333
16RMS MAR-DEC
T/T PETS CC KIDS
LOTS

16km from Taynuilt signed from A85. Rambling gothic mansion in sheltered landscaped gdns o/looking an enchanting loch. Genuine 'faux' grand that works. Deer wander outside and bats flap at dusk. Pure romance. Chef Gary Goldie deserves more credit perhaps, than he gets.

Ballathie House

Kinclaven
01250 883268
42RMS JAN-DEC
T/T PETS CC KIDS
LOTS

Superb situation on R Tay. 20km N of Perth via Blairgowrie rd A93/left follow signs after 16km just before the famous beech hedge; or A9 and 4km N, take B9000 through Stanley. Former baronial hunting lodge beside the R Tay. Relaxed and informal atmos in definitive country house. New riverside rms. Kevin MacGillivray's award-winning food. Fishing by arrangement with Estate office.

Sandford Hill

Nr Wormit
01382 541802
16RMS JAN-DEC
T/T PETS CC KIDS
EXP

7km S of Tay Bridge via A92 and A914, 100m along B946 to Wormit. An austere mansion with unusual layout and mullioned windows looking out to gorgeous gdns. Wild but romantic tennis court (someday they must get it back in use), pub lunches. 750 acres adj farmland of 'activities' – clay-pigeon shooting, fishing in Farm Loch, off-road driving.

Corrour House

Aviemore
01479 810220
8RMS JAN-DEC
T/T PETS CC KIDS
MED.EX

Small country house 3km from Aviemore on Coylumbridge rd, handy for the ski slopes. Without airs but not without graces, this family-run hotel is decent value. More like a GH with chef. Young deer in the gdn at daybreak, fine-size rms. Has changed hands a bit since original vision.

Crieff Hydro

Crieff
01764 655555
213RMS
(+SELF-CAT)
JAN-DEC T/T
PETS CC KIDS
MED.INX

A national institution & still a family business; your family is part of theirs. App via High St; follow signs. Vast Victorian pile with activities for all from bowlers to babies. Continuous refurbs, incl the fabulous winter gdns moving graciously with the times. Formal dining rm & the Brasserie (open all day). Gr tennis courts, riding school, Lagoon Pool. Tiny cinema shows family movies; nature talks, donkey rides. Kids endlessly entertained (even as you eat). Chalets are among the best in Scotland. Gr for family get-togethers.

Isles Of Glencoe Hotel

Ballachulish
01855 811602
59RMS
JAN-DEC T/T
PETS CC KIDS
MED.INX/EXP

By the A82 Crianlarich-Ft William: a modern hotel and leisure centre jutting out onto L Leven. Adventure playground outside and nature trails. Conservatory restau o/looking the water. Hotel has pool. 2 diff standards of family rms. Snacks in the restau all day. Lochaber Watersports next door, Glencoe and 2 ski areas nearby.

Scarista House

Harris
01859 550238
5RMS JAN-DEC
X/X PETS CC
KIDS EXP

20 mins S of Tarbert on W coast of S Harris, 45 mins Stornoway. Big, comfortable farmhouse o/looking amazing beach; also golf course. Lots of gr countryside around. The Martins have 3 school-age kids & yours may muck in with them (incl 6pm supper). Laid-back but civilised ambience.

Baile-Na-Cille

Timsgarry, Lewis
01851 672242
7RMS APR-OCT
X/X PETS CC
KIDS MED.INX

Far far into the sunset on the W of Lewis 60km Stornoway so a plane/ferry & drive to somewhere you can leave it all behind. Exquisite, vast beach, garden, tennis, games rm. No TV/phone/mobile. Plenty of books. The kids will never forget it.

Glenfinnan House

Glenfinnan
01397 722235
13RMS MAR-NOV
X/X PETS CC
KIDS MED.INX-EXP

Just off the 'Road to the Isles' (the A830 from Ft William to Mallaig). V large Highland 'hoose' with so many rms and such large gdns you can be as noisy as you like. Great intro to the Highland heartland; music, scenery and local characters. Cruise of the loch leaves from the foot of the lawn. Midge-eater in the garden.

Old Pines

Nr Spean Bridge
01397 712324
8RMS JAN-DEC
X/X XPETS CC
KIDS MED.INX

3km Spean Br via B8004 for Gairlochy at Commando Monument. A ranch-like hotel in a good spot N of Ft William. Previous owners the Barbours forged a big reputation for food and for a hotel that welcomed kids. New owners the Dalleys have (little) kids too & seem set to continue the laid-back & accommodating app. Separate mealtimes & with real food for kids.

Polmaily House

Nr
Drumnadrochit
01456 450343
10RMS + 2SUITES
JAN-DEC T/T
PETS CC KIDS
MED.EX

5km from L Ness rd at Drumnadrochit via A831 to Cannich, a good co-house hotel for adults that is excellent for kids. Lots to do in the gdns: trout pond where older kids can fish, pet rabbit run, bikes, indoor swimming pool, pool room. Tree house & swing up the back esp popular. Separate kids' meal time; special rates.

Peebles Hydro

Peebles
01721 720602
128RMS JAN-DEC
T/T PETS CC KIDS
MED.INX/EXP

Innerleithen Rd. One of the first Victorian hydros, now more Butlins than Bath. Huge grounds, corridors (you get lost) and floors of rms where kids can run around. Pool & leisure facs. Entertainment and baby-sitting services. V traditional and refreshingly untrendy. Rms vary. Dining rm is vast; Lazels bistro downstairs is light, contemporary and unnecessarily good.

The Cally Palace

*Gatehouse Of
Fleet*
01557 814341
*56RMS JAN-DEC
T/T PETS CC KIDS
MED.EX*

The big all-round family & golf hotel in the SW in charming vill with walks & beaches nearby. Leisure facs incl pool & tennis. 500 acres of forested grounds. 9 family rms.

Stonefield Castle Hotel

Tarbert, Argyll
01880 820836
*33RMS JAN-DEC
T/T PETS CC KIDS
MED.EX*

Just outside town on the A83, a castle which evokes the 1970s more than preceding centuries. Splendid luxuriant gdns leading down to L Fyne. 60 acres of woody grounds to explore. Dining-rm with baronial splendour and staggering views. Friendly, flexible staff; overall, it seems quintessentially Scottish and ok, esp for families though the style police would have words. Most deals incl dinner too.

Hilton Coylumbridge

Nr Aviemore
01479 810661
*175 (INCL
FAMILY)RMS
JAN-DEC T/T PETS
CC KIDS LOTS*

8km from Aviemore Centre on B970 rd to ski slopes and nearest hotel to them. 2 pools of decent size, sauna, flume, etc. Plenty to do in summer and winter and certainly where to go when it rains. Best of the often-criticised Aviemore concrete blocks, the most facs, huge new shed with kids' play area (the 'Funhouse'), staff wandering around in animal costumes, kids' mealtimes & even prog.

Calgary Hotel

Nr Dervaig, Mull
01688 400256
9RMS MAR-NOV
X/X PETS CC
KIDS MED.INX

20km S Tobermory (& a long way from Balamory), a roadside farmhouse/bistro/gallery, ie v laid-back place. Main features are beautiful wood out back (with art in it, but an adventure land for kids) & Mull's famously fab beach adj. 2 gr family rms.

Waterside Inn

Peterhead
01779 471121
109(16FAMILY)RMS
JAN-DEC T/T
PETS CC KIDS
MED.EX

Edge of town on A952 to Fraserburgh. Modern hotel with pool etc and some activities for kids. Aden Country Park nearby. Kids' meal and playrm 7-9pm while you eat, and family rms. Ugie and Deedee (the bears) are a gr success, but you wouldn't want to take them to bed. Adventure playground. Go-karts. Sometimes special family w/ends.

Philipburn

Selkirk
01750 720747
17RMS JAN-DEC
T/T PETS CC KIDS
EXP

1km from town centre on A707 Peebles Rd. Excl hotel for families, walkers, week-end away from it all. Selkirk is a good Borders base. Restaurant and bar-bistro and rare outdoor pool (with 2 family rms o/looking). Comfy rms, some luxurious. Best vegn food for miles around here.

The Three Chimneys

Colbost, Skye
01470 511258
8RMS JAN-DEC
T/T PETS CC KIDS
LOTS

7km W of Dunvegan on B884 to Glendale. Rms in a new build across the yard from the excl Three Chimneys restau called **The House Over-by**. Roadside tho few cars and within sight and smell of the sea. Good standard split-level rms with own doors to the sward. Breakfast lounge, s/serv v healthy buffet. A model of its kind, so often full. Be sure to book for dinner!

Glenelg Inn

Glenelg
01599 522273
6RMS (+1)
JAN-DEC X/X
PETS XCC KIDS
MED.EXP

Almost at the end of that gr rd over the hill from Shiel Br on the A87 is the civilised hostelry of the irrepressible Chris Main. Decent food, good drinking, snug lounge. Gdn with tables and views. Charming rms. Chris's wife's pictures adorn the walls & his boat *Blossom* may take you to Sandaig or elsewhere on this mystic coast. Yvonne cooks Tues-Sat. Adj cottage (rm7) avail. From Glenelg, take the best route to Skye.

Argyll Hotel

Iona
01681 700334
16RMS
EASTER-NOV
X/X PETS CC
KIDS MED.INX

On beautiful, turquoise bay betw Iona & Mull on rd betw ferry & abbey. Daytrippers come & go but stay! A charming hotel & a remarkable island. Cosy rms (1 suite), good food (esp vegn) fresh from the organic garden. The real peace & quiet and that's just sitting on the bench outside. It's Colourist country; they would have stayed here too.

Applecross Inn

Applecross
01520 744262
7RMS JAN-DEC
X/X PETS CC
KIDS INX

The legendary end of the rd, this waterside inn is a haven of hospitality. Buzzes all seasons. Rms small (1+7 best). Judy Fish & a gr team & a real chef look after you. Poignant VC, walled garden, lovely walks and even a real pizza hut in summer to keep you happy in Applecross for days.

Craw Inn

Auchencrow
01890 761253
3RMS JAN-DEC
X/X PETS CC
XKIDS INX

5 km A1 and well worth short detour into Berwickshire countryside. Quintessential inn with cosy pub & dining rm. Funky furniture, simple rms. Food decent, wines extraordinary.

The Stein Inn

Waternish, Skye
01470 592362
5RMS JAN-DEC
X/X PETS CC
KIDS CHP

Off B886 the Dunvegan-Portree rd, about 10km Dunvegan. In row of cottages on waterside. The 'oldest inn on Skye' with gr pub (open fire, good grub) & comfortable small rms above. Gr value in a special spot. Excl seafood restau adj.

Plockton Hotel

Plockton
01599 544274
11RMS JAN-DEC
T/T XPETS CC
KIDS MED.INX

On shoreline of one of Scotland's most picturesque vills. Dreamy little bay. Many visitors & this pub gets busy, but food is great & rms upstairs are recently refurb & not without charm.

West Loch Hotel

Tarbert
01880 820283
8RMS JAN-DEC
X/T PETS CC KIDS
MED.INX

Beside A83 just W of Tarbert; reasonable inx stopover en route to the islands. Comfortably furnished; with some original features. Board games and books dotted around, children welcome in relaxed, friendly atmos. Good value, but roadside rms may be noisy.

Old Inn

Gairloch
01445 712006
15RMS JAN-DEC
T/T PETS CC KIDS
MED.INX

Southern app on A832, tucked away by river and 'old bridge'. Excl pub for food, music (traditional & contemporary nights Tue/Fri). A recent 'pub of the year'. Nice, simple rms (tho' the pub goes like a fair). Routinely rec in pub guides.

Kilberry Inn

Nr Tarbert, Argyll
01880 770223
3RMS MAR-DEC
X/T PETS CC
KIDS MED.INX

Half-way round the Knapdale peninsula on the single-track B8024, the long way to Lochgilphead. Homely roadside inn with simple inex rms & excl cooking. A gem.

Cairnbaan Hotel

Cairnbaan nr
Lochgilphead
01546 603668
12RMS JAN-DEC
T/T PETS CC KIDS
MED.INX

Main attraction here is the location o/looking lochs of the Crinan Canal – nice to watch or walk (all the way to Crinan) if not messing about on a boat yourself. Decent pubgrub in or out & less success-ful dinner menu. Some ales.

Pier House

Port Appin
01631 730302
12RMS JAN-DEC
T/T XPETS
CC KIDS
MED.INX/MED.EX

An inn at the end of the rd (the minor rd that leads off the A828 Oban to Ft William) and at the end of the 'pier', where the tiny passenger ferry leaves for Lismore. Bistro restau with decent seafood in gr setting. Comfy motel-type rms (more exp o/look the sea & island) & conservatory restau & lounge. Gr place to take kids.

Glenisla Hotel

Kirkton Of
Glenisla
01575 582223
6RMS JAN-DEC
X/X PETS CC
KIDS MED.INX

20km NW of Kirriemuir via B951 at head of this secluded story-book glen. A home from home: hearty food, real ale & local colour. Fishers, stalkers, trekkers & walkers all come by. Miles from the town literally and laterally. Neat rms; convivial bar (sometimes live music).

Meikleour Hotel

Meikleour
01250 883206
5RMS JAN-DEC
X/T PETS CC
KIDS MED.EX

Just off the A93 Perth-Blairgowrie rd (on the B984) by the famously high beech hedge (a Perthshire icon). Roadside inn with quiet accom & food in dining rm or (more atmos) the bar. Deals going.

Bridge Of Orchy Hotel

Bridge Of Orchy
01838 400208
10RMS JAN-DEC
T/T PETS CC KIDS
MED.INX

Unmissable on the A82 (the rd to Glencoe, Ft William and Skye) 11km N of Tyndrum. Old inn extensively refurbished and run as a stopover hotel. Simple, quite stylish rms. A la carte menu & specials in pub/conservatory. Good spot for the malt on the W Highland Way. Also bunkhouse (v chp).

Cluanie Inn

Glenmoriston
01320 340238
12RMS+BUNKHSE
JAN-DEC T/X
PETS CC KIDS
INX-MED.EX

On main rd to Skye 15km before Shiel Br, a traditional inn surrounded by summits that attract walkers & travellers: the 5 Sisters, the Ridge & the Saddle. Club house adj has some group accom while inn rms can be high-spec – one with sauna, one with jacuzzi! Bar food LO 9pm. Bunkhouse basic & rms do vary. Friendly staff.

Traquair Arms

Innerleithen
01896 830229
20RMS JAN-DEC
T/T PETS CC KIDS
MED.INX

100m from the A72 Gala-Peebles rd towards Traquair, a popular village and country inn that caters for all kinds of folk (and, at w/ends, large numbers of them). Notable for bar meals, real ale and family facs. Rms refurb. Nice gdn out back. All food v home-made. New owners at time of going to print & additional rms imminent.

The Kames Hotel

Tighnabruaich
01700 811489
10RMS JAN-DEC
X/T PETS CC KIDS
MED.INX

Frequented by passing yachtsmen who moor alongside and pop in for lunch. Good base for all things offshore; marine cruises or a nostalgic journey on a 'puffer', with a gr selection of malts to warm you up before or after. Hotel on a rolling refurb, keen to be seen as an inn with rms. Gr bar tho' the famous lock-ins are over.

The Ceilidh Place

Ullapool
01854 612103
23RMS JAN-DEC
T/X PETS CC KIDS
EXP/CHP

Inimitable Jean Urquhart's place encapsulates Scottish traditional culture & hospitality & interprets it in a contemporary manner. Caters for all sorts: there's an excellent hotel above; a bistro/bar below (occasional live music & ceilidh-style performance); and a bunkhouse across the way with cheap & cheerful accom. Scottish-ness is all here & nothing embarrassing in sight.

The Albannach

Lochinver
01571 844407
5RMS MAR-DEC
T/X XPETS CC
XKIDS MED.INX

2km outside Lochinver on A837, at the br. Lovely 18thC house in one of Scotland's most scenic areas, Assynt, where the mtns can take your breath away even without going up them. The outbuilding o/looking the croft gives extra privacy & space. Rms being turned into gorgeous suites at time of going to print. Unwind in tasteful, informal surroundings. Food is the best for miles.

Kildrummy Castle Hotel

Nr Alford
01975 571288
16RMS FEB-DEC
T/T PETS CC KIDS
LOTS

60km W of Aberdeen via A944 lies this comfortable chunk of Scottish Baronial in a spectacular location with real Highlands aura. Well placed if you're on the 'Castle Trail'. The redolent ruins of Kildrummy Castle stand on the opposite bluff & a gorgeful of gdns betw. Some rms small, but all v Scottish. Jacket & tie for dinner.

Eilean Iarmain

Skye
01471 833332
12RMS+4SUITES
JAN-DEC T/T
PETS CC KIDS
EXP/LOTS

Sleat area on S of island, this snug Gaelic inn nestles in the bay and is the classic island hostelry. A dram in your rm awaits you; from the adj whisky company. Bedrms in hotel best but cottage annex quieter. New suites in adj steading more exp but nice. Food real good in d-rm or pub. Mystic shore walks.

Glenfinnan House

Glenfinnan
01397 722235
17RMS APR-OCT
X/X PETS CC KIDS
MED.INX-EXP

Off the Road to the Isles (A830 Ft William to Mallaig). The MacFarlanes have been running their legendary hotel in this historic house for 30 yrs. Ongoing refurb under the Gibsons retains its charm; the huge rms remain intimate & cosy with open fires. Impromptu sessions & ceilidhs wherever there's a gathering in the bar. Solitude achievable in the huge grounds, or fishing or dreaming on L Shiel (boat avail 01687 470322). Day trips to Skye & small islands nearby. Quintessential!

Savoy Park

Ayr
01292 266112
15RMS JAN-DEC
T/T PETS KIDS
MED.INX

In an area of many indifferent hotels this one, owned and run by the Henderson family for over 40 yrs, is a real Scottish gem. Many weddings here. Period features, lovely gdn, not too much tartan, but a warm cosy lived-in atmos. Round one of the fireplaces, 'blessed be God for his giftis'. Good place to stop for the Burns Festival in May.

The Carnegie Club

Skibo Castle,
Dornoch
01862 894600
21RMS(11LODGES)
JAN-DEC T/T
XPETS CC KIDS
LOTS AND LOTS

Not a hotel, they stress, but listen up! Just over Dornoch Br on A9 at Clashmore. A vast estate once home to the formidable Andrew Carnegie. Now it's a club for members only; you can sample the atmos once, say for a w/end, but to return you join the club. Some club! The sumptuous castle retains its original furnishings (silk wallpaper, panelling, etc.) and the service from your discreet 'hosts' is exemplary. Lodges in the grounds offer more privacy, with the obligatory 2 golf courses, spa, gym, pool and 'beach', all oases of relaxing indulgence – vintage Rolls Royces take you around. Many dining options. Everything here has a plus factor.

Monachyle Mhor

Nr Balquhidder
01877 384622
5+5RMS+2
COTT JAN-DEC
T/T PETS CC KIDS
MED.INX

Negotiate the thread of rd alongside L Voil from Balquhidder (11km from the A84 Callander-Crianlarich). Farmhouse o/looks L Voil from magnificent Balquhidder Braes. Friendly, cosy and inexpensive; a place to relax in summer or winter. New deluxe rms in house are best (twin baths, anyone?). Fishing. Food fairly fab, well-sourced ingredients, 2 AA rosettes. Tastefully done, gr informal atmos.

Ardeonaig

Loch Tay
01567 820400
20RMS JAN-DEC
T/X PETS CC
KIDS
MED.EX-LOTS

On narrow and scenic S Loch Tay rd midway betw Kenmore and Killin. An airy roadside inn by the water opposite Ben Lawers. South African chef/prop making the most of this perfectly remote location. Stylish rms, gr bar & excl dining with top urban standard of service. And friendly! Upstairs library with cool books and dreamy view of the Ben. Love that loch!

Loch Torridon

Nr Kinlochewe
01445 791242
19RMS JAN-DEC
T/T XPETS CC
XKIDS LOTS

Impressive former hunting lodge on loch-side, surrounded by majestic mts. A cosy, family-run baronial house with relaxed atmos. For all that, it also focuses on outdoor activities like clay-pigeon shoots, mountain bikes or fishing. Lots of walking possibilities. Gr malts in the dwindling day.

Tiroran House

Isle Of Mull
01681 705232
6RMS+2COTT
MAR-NOV X/T
XPETS CC KIDS
EXP

SW corner on rd to Iona from Craignure then B8035 round L na Keal. Family-friendly small co house in fabulous gdns by the sea, being refurb under new owners Laurence Mackay & Katie Munro (Katie a Cordon Bleu cook). Nr Iona & Ulva ferry; you won't miss Tobermory. Excl food from sea & kitchen gdn. Lovely rms. Sea eagles fly over, otters in the bay.

Moor Of Rannoch Hotel

Rannoch Station
01882 633238
5RMS JAN-DEC
X/X PETS CC
KIDS MED.INX

Beyond Pitlochry and the Trossachs and far W via L Tummel and L Rannoch (B8019 and B8846) so a wonderful journey to the edge of Rannoch Moor & adj station so you could get the sleeper from London & be here for b/fast. 4 trains either way ea day via Glasgow. Literally the end of the road but an exceptional find in the middle of nowhere. Cosy, wood-panelled rms, great restau (open to non-residents). Quintessential Highland Inn. Gr walking.

Glen Clova Hotel

Nr Kirriemuir
01575 550350
10RMS JAN-DEC
T/T XPETS CC
KIDS MED.INX

25km N of Kirriemuir to head of glen on B955; once you're there there's nowhere to go but up. Rms all en-suite & surprisingly well appointed. Climbers' bar (till all hrs). Superb walking hereabouts (e.g. L Brandy). A laid-back get-away tho lots of families drive up on a Sun for lunch.

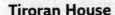

Great Get-Away-From-It-All Hotels

Corsewall Lighthouse Hotel

Nr Stranraer
01776 853220
7RMS (+ SUITES IN GROUNDS)
JAN-DEC T/T
PETS CC KIDS
EXP

Only 15mins from Stranraer (via A718 to Kirkcolm) and follow signs, but way up on the peninsula and as it suggests a hotel made out of a working lighthouse. Romantic and offbeat, decent food too, and there are attractions nearby esp at Portpatrick 30 mins away thro the maze of quiet backroads.

Mackays

Durness
01971 511202
7RMS JAN-DEC
X/T XPETS CC
KIDS MED.INX

Remote from rest of Scotland (the top NW corner) but actually in centre of township. Many interesting distractions nearby. A comfortable, contemporary restau with rms. Wood & slate: the coolest retreat in the N. Gr food.

Corriechoille Lodge

By Spean Bridge
01397 712002
5RMS MAR-OCT
X/T XPETS CC
KIDS INX

3km from S Bridge via rd by station. Lovely rd & spectacularly situated; it's great to arrive. Justin & Lucy share their perfect retreat with you. Spectacular views towards the Grey Corries & Aonach Mor. Lovely dinner, cosy rms. 2 turf-roofed self-cat chalets over by. Gt walks begin here.

Glenmorangie House

Cadboll nr Fearn
01862 871671
9RMS JAN-DEC
T/X XPETS CC
XKIDS EXP

S of Tain 10km E of A9. Old whisky mansion in open grounds o/look sea recently taken over by Louis Vuitton Moët Hennessy so expect some luxury (tho' everything is understated). No leisure facs but no shortage of distraction around. Return to comfy rms, open fires & communal, house-party atmos. Chef has good reputation. Fixed dinner round one table, honesty bar, gr service.

Tomdoun Hotel

Nr Invergarry
01809 511218
10RMS JAN-DEC
X/X PETS CC
KIDS INX

20km from Invergarry, 12km off the A87 to Kyle of Lochalsh. This 19thC coaching inn replaced a much older one; off the beaten track but perfect for fishing & walking (L Quoich and Knoydart, the last wilderness, have been waiting for you). Superb views over Glengarry and Bonnie Prince Charlie's country. House-party atmos, mix-match furniture & nice dogs. Real chef with meticulously sourced seafd menu.

The Pier House

Inverie, Knoydart
01687 462347
4RMS MAR-OCT
X/X XPETS XCC
KIDS CHP

Currently the only restau on this far-away peninsula, tho good grub at the pub nearby. Accessible on foot from Kinlochourn (25km) or Bruce Watt's boat from Mallaig (01687 462320). Friendly couple offer warm hospitality in their home and surprisingly good cooking for somewhere so remote; rovers often return.

Doune Stone Lodge

Knoydart
01687 462667
6RMS(+12)
APR-SEP X/X
XPETS CC KIDS
MED.INX

As above, on remote Knoydart & this gr spot on the W tip o/looking a bay on the Sound of Sleat. They have own boats so pick you up from Mallaig & drop you round the inlets for walking. Otherwise 8km from Inverie. Rms & lodge for 12. Own restau. Only lodge avail in wint.

Tomich Hotel

Nr Cannich
01456 415399
8RMS JAN-DEC
T/T PETS CC KIDS
MED.INX

8km from Cannich which is 25km from Drumnadrochit. Fabulous Plodda Falls are nearby. Cosy country inn in conservation village with added bonus of use of swimming pool in nearby steading. Faraway feel, surprising bar round the back. Good base for outdoorsy w/end. Glen Affric across the way.

Skippers

0131 554 1018
1a Dock Pl, Leith.
Lunch & dinner 7
days, LO 10pm.
MED

In a corner of Leith off Commercial Rd by the docks. Bistro with truly maritime atmos; mainly seafood. Many would argue Skippers *is* still the best place to eat seafood in this town. Small & many-chambered; v quayside intimate & friendly. Excl apt wine list. Best to book.

Fishers In The City

0131 225 5109
58 Thistle St.
7 days. LO
10.30pm.
MED

Uptown version of one of Leith's longest best eateries (below); this place works on all its levels (we're talking mezzanine). Fisher fan staples ('favourites') all here – the fishcakes, the soup & the blackboard specials, excl wine list combined with gr service Some vegn & meat (steaks a special). Open all day (reduced menu late aft).

Fishers

0131 554 5666
Corner of The
Shore & Tower St,
Leith.
7 days. 12noon-
10pm.
MED

At the foot of an 18thC tower opposite Malmaison Hotel and rt on the quay (though no boats come by). Seafood cooking with flair and commitment in boat-like surroundings where traditional Scots dishes get an imaginative twist. Hugely popular, some stools around bar and tables outside in summer (can be a windy corner). Often, all are packed. Cheeseboard has some gr Brits if you have rm for a third course.

Big Fish

0131 556 6655
14 Bonnington
Rd nr Gt Jnctn St.
Alternate Fri &
Sat dinner only (cl
in wint).

MED

Occasional restau in 'The Commissary', James Robb's dining rm & kitchen used for private parties & to prepare outside catering for Edin's poshest parties. Big Fish an Edin secret & real treat. Windowless but light rm illuminated by projected film. Freshest of fish & personalised cooking options. Starters & puds just delicious. Booking a must.

Creelers

0131 220 4447
3 Hunter Sq.
Lunch & LO
10.30/11pm (not
Tues/Wed lunch
in wint).

MED

Tim & Fran's restau & smoke house near Brodick is also called Creelers. This corner of Arran in the city behind the Tron Church is just a short cast from the Royal Mile (tables alfresco in summer). Nice wine list. Fish served pure & simple. Some supplies from their own boat & Arran (hand-dived) scallops. Nice paintings, good atmos & new chef '05.

The Mussel Inn

0131 225 5979
61 Rose St.
Lunch & dinner.
LO 10pm.

INX

Popular, populist. In the heart of the city centre where parking ain't easy, a gr little seafood bistro specializing in mussels and scallops (kings and queens) which the proprietors rear/find themselves. Also catch of the day, some non-fish options & home-made puds. This formula could travel but the owners have wisely decided not to travel far – they're also in Glas.

Roti

0131 225 1233
70 Rose St Ln N.
Tues-Sat, dinner
only LO 11pm.
MED

Central yet discreet location for this simple, small rm (& bar annex) with superb Indian food – tho prop Tony Singh insists this is not 'an Indian restaurant'. Magic combos of flavours & lots of lightness: an ethnic cuisine at its best.

The Original Khushi's

0131 667 0888
26 Potterow.
7 days lunch &
dinner. LO 11pm.
INX

Long regarded as the only real Indian kitchen, this basic Punjabi café has drawn in students and others since Nehru was in his collar, or at least in the news. Almost feels like a trattoria but definitively Indian. May have to book. Must BYOB.

Suruchi

0131 556 6583
14a Nicolson St.
Lunch (not Sun) &
LO 11.30pm daily.
INX

Eclectic Indian menu written touchingly in Scots dialect. Unfussy if somewhat worn décor & food with light touch attracts students/academics from nearby university as well as theatregoers. Loads for veggies. Better than av wines. **Suruchi Too** at 121 Constitution St, Leith (554 3268).

Kalpna

0131 667 9890
St Patrick Sq.
Mon-Sat. Lunch
& LO 10.30pm.
INX

The original Edin Indian veggie restau & still the business. Lighter, fluffier & not as attritional as so many tandooris. Some unique dishes. Gujarati menu. Long may it prevail.

Namaste

0131 225 2000
15 Bristo Pl.
7 days, dinner
only LO 10/11pm.
MED

The new place on the block for those that want care in the curry. Authentic N Indian cuisine incl currys prod in traditional brass pot! Familiar faves, light nans in a rm round the corner from the univ and the rest of the crazy world.

Britannia Spice

0131 555 2255
150 Commercial St.
7 days, lunch LO 11.30pm.
MED

Nr Ocean Terminal & the royal yacht Britannia. Widespread menu from the sub-continent served by quietly efficient waiters in modern maritime setting. Some awards, some suits.

Kebab Mahal

0131 667 5214
7 Nicolson Sq.
7 days noon-midnight (2am Fri/Sat).
CHP

Gr vegetable biryani and delicious lassi for under a fiver? Hence high cult status. Late-night Indo-Pakistani halal caff attracts Asian families, students and others who know. Kebabs, curries and fab sweets. Prayers 1-2pm Fri. No-alcohol zone.

The Khukuri

0131 228 2085
8 W Maitland St.
7 days lunch & LO 11pm (cl Sun lunch).
INX

Unassuming Nepalese restau is a quiet secret. Chef Dharma Mahrajan routinely wins awards & brings the herbs himself from the mountains of Nepal. Massive menu & mellow atmos, but meat-eaters (lamb & chicken) will be happiest here.

The Raj

0131 553 3980
89 Henderson St.
Lunch & LO 11.30pm, 7 days.
INX

Nice Leith location for the irrepressible Tommy Miah's airy Indian/Bangladeshi restau. Here some yrs now, but still bustling & still changing. Occasional events add to the jollity; jars of things to buy and take home, also recipe books. Tables best on the raised front area.

Ann Purna

0131 662 1807
45 St Patrick Sq.
Lunch Mon-Fri, dinner 7 days, LO 10.30pm.
INX

Excellent vegn restau nr Edin University with genuine Gujarati cuisine. Good atmos - old customers are greeted like friends by Mr & Mrs Pandya. Indian beer, some suitable wines. Seriously value-for-money business lunch & lovely, harmonious food at all times.

Dragonfly

0131 228 4543
West Port.
7 days till midnight.

Discreet frontage conceals a more beautiful, more stylish world where alcohol is treated like food in a fine restau & cocktails are king. Lofty rm with mezzanine. Not many distractions from the aesthetic.

Opal Lounge

0131 226 2275
51a George St.
Admn & queue
after 10pm. Open
till 3am 7 days.

Basement in Edin's fashion mile for not-so-new 'lifestyle' project from the indigo (yard) stable (see below). Sunken, sexy lounges incl dancefloor and restau (fusion tho not what they do best). Gr staff know how to serve cocktails. Big door presence.

Villager

0131 226 2781
50 George IV Br.
Bar till 1am.

Nr University & Nat Library a funked-up, laid-back place to hang out. DJs (Fri/Sat), OK pub food till 9.30 but mainly the right faces in a photo from 2005 and maybe '06.

The Outhouse

0131 557 6668
12a Broughton St
Lane.
Bar till 1am.

Happily mixed & unobtrusive modern bar off Broughton St off the Pink Triangle. Modish food 12noon-7pm (4pm w/ends) for self-conscious business diners. Gr Sun BBQ out back in summer.

The Street

0131 556 4272
2 Picardy Pl.
7 days till 1am.

Corner glass box at the top of Broughton St in the Pink Triangle; so gay-friendly. Gr people-watching spot. DJs w/ends. Madame (Trendy) Wendy & gals in charge.

indigo (yard)

0131 220 5603
7 Charlotte Lane,
off Queensferry
St.
7 days till 1am.

Long-est spacious kinda-'90s café-bar offers exposed brickwork, balcony tables, booths and babes in blue of both genders serving good food and drink. More Med than Mex cuisine with flexible menu.

Rick's

0131 622 7800
55a Frederick St.
Till 1am.

Another café-bar-restau by the Opal/indigo people, this time with rms. Bar service gd & they know how to mix cocktails. Eating experience drowned out later.

Left Bank

0131 445 2977
37 Guthrie St.
11pm-3am.

V boho, Festival Fringe-like: gr atmos, cool late-night people. Live music in cavernous 'Alba' room. Go dig!

The Pond

Corner of
Bath Rd &
Salamander St,
Leith.

So cool it's the opposite of a style bar, a million miles from George St. The people here don't want to be hip; they want to watch fish & swing in the basket chair.

Boda Bar

Corner of Leith
Walk & Lorne St.
Bar till 1am
(midnight Sun).

Swedish import, v welcome on the Walk. Boda a small village in N Sweden, & this has village feel. Friendly staff. Well-chosen fare incl snax (moose sausages anyone?). Sister bar, **Sofi's**, further into Leith (Henderson St).

Iglu

Jamaica St off
Howe St.
4pm-1am
(Fri/Sat from 12).

Surprisingly cool bar in conservative territory. Small upstairs garret with nice fish tank. Very Edinburgh, kind of lovely!

City Café

0131 220 0127
19 Blair St.
11am-1am.

A true original that went from *the* hippest, to nowhere, and now back again with cool night people. Buzzing at the w/ends. DJs downstairs. Pool tables never stop.

Roastit Bubbly Jocks

0141 339 3355
450 Dumbarton
Rd.
Lunch Fri-Sun.
LO 10pm. Cl
Mon.
INX

Far up in the W End but many beat their way to this Partick dining rm where Mo Abdulla has expanded his cosy wee empire but kept it well... cosy & excl value. Not so much 'Scottish' as Scottish sourced (ingredients) & presented (couthy ambience). And things we Scots like incl Irish stew & pavlova. Can BYO.

Arisaig

0141 204 5399
140 St Vincent St.
7 days, LO
9.30/10.30pm.
INX

A stylish, smartly presented Scottish bistro inspired by the area where Arisaig lies on the Road to the Isles. Well sourced ingredients from 'Sea and Land'. Good vegn choice. Big portions. More claim to be presenting contemporary Scotland food, ingredients & culture than others that have clambered on bandwagon.

City Merchant

0141 553 1577
97 Candleriggs.
7 days lunch &
dinner (not Sun
lunch).
INX

One of the first restaus in the Merchant City & longevity in Glas attests to enduring appeal. 'Seafood, game, steaks' focussing on quality Scottish produce with daily & à la carte menus in warm bistro atmos. Good biz restau or intimate rendezvous.

Babbity Bowster

16 Blackfriars St.

Noted as a pub for real ale and as a hotel (rms upstairs), the food is notable mainly for its Scottishness (haggis and stovies) and all-day availability. It's also pleasant to eat outside on the patio/gdn in summer. Restau upstairs (dinner only Tues-Sat) but we prefer down. Also breakfast served from 8am (Sun 10am).

The Horseshoe

17 Drury St.
Pub open daily
till 12 midnight.

This classic pub to be recommended for all kinds of reasons. But lunch is a particularly good deal with 3 courses for £2.80 (pie & beans still 80p), and old favourites on the menu like mushy peas, macaroni cheese, jelly and fruit. Lunch 12noon-2.30pm. Upstairs open all aft, then for high tea till 6.30pm (not Sun) (not quite the same atmos, but pure Glas). 4-course meal for £4.95 at time of going to print. All Glas faves.

The Bothy

0141 334 4040
11 Ruthven Lane.
7 days noon-10pm.

INX

Part of Stefan King's Gl Group's takeover of the W End, this tucked-away site has housed several restaus of note. This latest reflects current return to roots, ie simpler, more comfort food from the gastrification of café-bar menus & the glorification of chefs. Contemporary-retro design is patchy but menu confidently conceived & presented. All-Scottish fare & notable ingredients all present & correct. We must hope standards keep up.

Òran Mór

Gt Western Rd at
Byres Rd.
Brasserie lunch
Wed-Sat; dinner
Mon-Sat.

MED

Huge & hugely popular pub emporium in converted church on prominent W End corner. A one-stop celebration of the parts of Scottish culture that go well with a drink, incls food, music, comedy, clubbing it & plays at lunchtime. The Brasserie is the upmarket-dining bit. Drinking on all levels. Big entertainment programme from DJs to comedy & 'A Play and a Pint'. They thought of everything.

Thai Lemongrass

0141 331 1315
24 Renfrew St.
7 days lunch &
LO 11.30pm.
MED

Noticing perhaps that Glas has far fewer good Thai restaus than Edin, Bruntsfield's has opened up here & become quite possibly the best in town. Contemp while still cosy. It seems set to give old Thai Fountain (below) a run for its baht. Good service & presentation of all the new Thai faves.

Thai Fountain

0141 332 2599
2 Woodside Cres.
Lunch and LO
11pm.
MED

Charing Cross, nr M8, Mitchell Library, etc. Tho old-style now this is still one of the best Thais in Scotland. Owned by Chinese Mr Chung but the Thai chefs know a green curry from a red. Tom yam excellent and weeping tiger beef v popular with those who really just want a steak. Lots of prawn and fish dishes and real vegn choice.

Thai Siam

0141 229 1191
1191 Argyle St (W
End Side).
Lunch & LO
11pm. Cl Sun
lunch.
MED

Traditional homely (if dimly lit) atmos but fashionable clientele who swear it has the prawniest crackers and greenest curry in town. Has moved on since prop/chef Pawina Kennedy sizzled the woks, but the all-Thai staff in kitchen & up front maintain authenticity.

Bar Gandolfi

0141 552 6813
64 Albion St
above Café
Gandolfi. 7 days
9am-11.30pm
(Sun from noon).

In a section where food counts as much as or more than the drink, Bar Gandolfi heads it up. A foody pub wih no pretence, just gr comfort food in a light, airy upstairs garret, served all day. Good veggie choice. Gr rendezvous spot.

Stravaigin

0141 334 2665
28-30 Gibson St.
7 days all day &
LO 10pm.

Excellent pub food upstairs from one of the best restaus in town. Doors open on to sunny and sorry Gibson St & mezzanine above. Crowded maybe, but inspirational grub & no fuss. Nice wines.

Liquid Ship

0141 331 1901
171 Gr Western
Rd. Bar 11/midnight. 7 days.

From the makers of Stravaigin (above), a newer venture on the highway to the W. Eclectic menu from Spain to the Ukraine & lots of Stravaigin touches as you'd expect. Food 11am-8pm (9 sometimes) then tapas menu till 10.30pm.

Bar Budda

0141 248 7881
142 St Vincent St;
337 6201,
Cresswell Lane.
Bar 11/12.

Burgeoning W coast chain, where food is surprisingly ok; surprising because Budda style might be expected to triumph over content. Modern menu mix, more Thai at night. Food till the throng takes over, usually 9pm (earlier Fri/Sat St Vincent St).

McPhabbs

0141 221 0770
22 Sandyford Pl.
Bar 11/midnight.

W of Sauchiehall St, other side of the m/way. Long-standing gr Glas pub with loyal following. Tables in front 'garden' & on narrow back deck. Standard homemade pubgrub menu. Food till 9pm. DJ Mark Robb from groovy Buff Club spun here at time of going to print.

Part 3

Scot land the best

The Best Places to Visit

Pete's Beach

nr Durness

One of many gr beaches on the N coast but this I've called my own. The hill above it is called 'Ceannabeinne'; you find it 7km E of Durness. Coming from Tongue it's just after where L Eriboll comes out to the sea & the rd hits the coast again (there's a layby opposite). It's a small perfect cove flanked by walls of coral-pink rock and shallow turquoise sea. Splendid from above (land rises to a bluff with a huge boulder) & from below. There's a bench – sit down next to me and leave your footprints in the sand. Excl inx GH nearby – **Port-Na-Con**.

Kiloran Beach

Colonsay

9km from quay and hotel, past Colonsay House: parking and access on hill side. Often described as the finest beach in the Hebrides, it does not disappoint tho' it has changed character in recent yrs (a shallower sandbar traps tidal run-off). Craggy cliffs on one side, negotiable rocks on the other and, in betw, tiers of grassy dunes. Do go to the end! The island of Colonsay was once bought as a picnic spot. This beach was probably the reason why.

Moray Coast

*Cullen,
Lossiemouth,
New Aberdour,
Rosehearty,
Sunnyside*

Many gr beaches along coast from Spey Bay to Fraserburgh, notably **Cullen** and **Lossiemouth** (town beaches) and **New Aberdour** (1km from New Aberdour village on B9031, 15km W of Fraserburgh) and **Rosehearty** (8km W of Fraserburgh) both quieter places for walks and picnics. One of the best-kept secrets is the beach at **Sunnyside** where you walk past the incredible ruins of Findlater Castle on the cliff top (how did they build it? A place, on its grassed-over roof, for a picnic) and down to a cove which on my sunny day was simply perfect. Take a left going into Sandend 16km W of Banff, follow rd for 2km, turn rt, park in the farmyard. Walk from here past dovecote, 1km to cliff. Also signed from A98.

Macrihanish

10km from Campbeltown

At the bottom of the Kintyre peninsula. Walk N from Machrihanish village or golf course, or from the car park on the main A83 to Tayinloan and Tarbert at pt where it hits/leaves the coast. A joyously long strand (8km) of unspoiled orange-pink sand backed by dunes and facing the 'steepe Atlantic Stream' all the way to Newfoundland.

Sandwood Bay

Kinlochbervie

This mile-long sandy strand with its old 'Stack', is legendary, but therein lies the problem since now too many people know about it and you may have to share in its glorious isolation. Inaccessibility is its saving grace, a 7km walk from the sign off the rd at Balchrick (nr the cattle grid), 6km from Kinlochbervie or cut a third of the distance in a 4-wheel drive; allow 3hrs return plus time there. More venturesome is the walk from the N and Cape Wrath. Managed by John Muir Trust. Go easy & go in summer! Also:

Oldshoremore

3km from Kinlochbervie

The beach you pass on the rd to Balchrick. It's easy to reach and a beautiful spot: the water is clear and perfect for swimming, and there are rocky walks and quiet places. **Polin**, 500m N, is a cove you might have to yourself.

Islay

Saligo, Machir Bay and The Big Strand

Saligo & Machir are bays on NW of island via A847 rd to Pt Charlotte, then B8018 past L Gorm. Wide beaches; remains of war fortifications in deep dunes, Machir perhaps best for beach bums. They say 'no swimming' so paddle with extreme prejudice. The Big Strand on Laggan Bay: along Bowmore-Pt Ellen rd take Oa t/off, follow Kintra signs. There's camping and gr walks in either direction, 8km of glorious sand and dunes. An airy amble under a wide sky.

Ostal Beach/Kilbride Bay

Millhouse nr Tighnabruaich

3km from Millhouse on B8000 signed Ardlamont (not Portvadie, the ferry), a track to rt before white house (often with a chain across to restrict access). Park and walk 1.5km, turning rt after lochan. You arrive on a perfect white sandy crescent known locally as Ostal and, apart from the odd swatch of sewage, in some conditions, a mystical secret place to swim and picnic.

South Uist

Deserted but for birds, an almost unbroken strand of beach running for miles down the W coast; the machair at its best early summer. Take any rd off the spinal A865; usually less than 2km. Good spot to try is t/off at Tobha Mor; real black houses and a chapel on the way to the sea.

Scarista Beach

South Harris

On main rd S of Tarbert (15km) to Rodel. The beach is so beautiful that people have been married there. Hotel over the rd is worth staying just for this, but is also a gr retreat. Golf course on links. Fab in early evening. The sun also rises.

Lunan Bay

Nr Montrose

5km from main A92 rd to Aber and 5km of deep red crescent beach under a wide northern sky. But'n'Ben, Auchmithie, is an excellent place to start or finish and good app (from S), although Gordon's restau at Inverkeilor is closer. Best viewpoint from Boddin Farm 3km S Montrose and 3km from A92 signed 'Usan'. Often deserted.

The Secret Beach

Nr Achmelvich

Can app from Achmelvich car park going N (it's the next proper bay round) or from Lochinver-Stoer/Drumbeg rd (less walk, layby on rt after Archmelvich t/off). Called **Alltan na Bradhan**, it's the site of an old mill (griding wheels still there), perfect for camping & the best sea for swimming. Sorry Colin & Leslie – hope you still have it to yourselves next summer.

Jura

Lowlandman's Bay

Not strictly a beach (there is a sandy strand before the headland) but a rocky foreshore with ethereal atmos; gr light and space. Only seals break the spell. Go rt at 3-arch br to first group of houses (Knockdrome), through yard on left and rt around cottages to track to Ardmenish. After deer fences, bay is visible on your rt, 1km walk away.

Vatersay

Outer Hebrides

The tiny island joined by a causeway to Barra. Twin crescent beaches on either side of the isthmus, one shallow and sheltered visible from Castlebay, the other an ocean beach with rollers. Dunes/machair; safe swimming. There's a helluva hill betw Barra and Vatersay if you're cycling.

Barra

Seal Bay

5km Castlebay on W coast, 2km after Isle of Barra Hotel through gate across machair where rd rt is signed Taobh a Deas Allathasdal. A flat, rocky Hebridean shore and skerries where seals flop into the water and eye you with intense curiosity. The better-beach beach is next to the hotel.

West Sands

St Andrews

As a town beach, this is hard to beat; it dominates the view to W. Wide swathe not too unclean and sea swimmable. Golf courses behind. Consistently gets 'blue flag' but beach buffs may prefer Kinshaldy, Kingsbarns (10km S) or Elie (28km S).

North Coast

Strathy,
Armadale, Farr,
Torrisdale,
Coldbackie

To the W of Thurso, along the N coast, are some of Britain's most unspoiled and unsung beaches. No beach bums, no Beach Boys. There are so many gr little coves, you can have one to yourself even on a hot day, but those to mention are: **Strathy** and **Armadale** (35km W Thurso), **Farr** and **Torrisdale** (48km) and **Coldbackie** (65km). My favourite is elevated to the top of this category.

Sands of Morar

Nr Mallaig

70km W of Ft William by newly improved rd, these beaches may seem overpopulated on summer days and the S stretch near Arisaig may have one too many caravan parks, but they go on for miles and there's enough space for everybody. The sand's supposed to be silver but in fact it's a v pleasing pink. Lots of rocky bits for exploration. One of the best beachy bits is 'Camusdaroch', signed from the main rd (where *Local Hero* was filmed).

The Bay At The Back Of The Ocean

Iona Easy 2km walk from frequent ferry from Fionnphort, S of Mull or hire a bike from the store on your left as you walk into the village (01681 700357). Paved rd most of way. John Smith, who is buried beside the abbey, once told me that this was one of his favourite places. There's a gr inx hotel on Iona, The Argyll.

Dornoch (& Embo Beaches)

Dornoch Firth The wide and extensive sandy beach of this pleasant town at the mouth of the Dornoch Firth famous also for its golf links. 4km N, Embo Sands starts with ghastly caravan city, but walk N towards Golspie. Embo is twinned with Kaunakakai, Hawaii!

Port Of Ness

Isle of Lewis Also signed Port Nis, this is the beach at the end of the Hebrides in the far N of Lewis. Just keep driving. There are some interesting stops on the way to this tiny bay & harbour down the hill at the end of the rd. Anthony Barber's Harbour View Gallery full of his own work (which you find in many other galleries & even postcards) is worth a visit (10am-5pm, cl Sun).

2 Beaches In The Far SW

Killantringan Bay and Sandhead Beach **Killantringan Bay nr Portpatrick** lies off the A77 before PP signed 'Dunskey Gardens' in summer. Foll rd signed Killantringan Lighthouse (dirt track). Park 1km before lighthouse. Beautiful bay for exploration. **Sandhead Beach** is by the A716 S of Stranraer. Shallow, safe waters of Luce Bay. Perfect for families. And thanks to Alison.

Glen Affric

Beyond Cannich at end of Glen Urquhart A831, 20km from Drumnadrochit on L Ness

A dramatic gorge that strikes westwards into the wild heart of Scotland. Superb for rambles, expeditions, Munro-bagging (further in, beyond L Affric) and even tootling through in the car. Shaped by the Hydro Board, L Benevean adds to the drama. Cycling good (bike hire in Cannich 01456 415251 & at the campsite) as is the detour to Tomich & Plodda Falls. Stop at Dog Falls.

Glen Lyon

Nr Aberfeldy

One of Scotland's crucial places historically and geographically, favoured by fishers/walkers/Munro-baggers. Wordsworth, Tennyson, Gladstone and Baden Powell all sang its praises. The Lyon, a classic Highland river, tumbles through corries, gorges & riverine meadows. Several Munros rise gloriously on either side. Rd all the way to the loch side (30km). Eagles soar over the remoter tops at the glen head. The PO coffee shop does a roaring trade.

Glen Nevis

Fort William

Used by many a film director; easy to see why. Ben Nevis is only part of magnificent scenery. Many walks & convenient facs. W Highland Way emerges here. Vis centre & cross river to climb Ben Nevis. Good caff in season. This woody, dramatic glen is a national treasure.

Glen Etive

Off from more exalted Glencoe (and the A82) at Kingshouse, as anyone you meet in those parts will tell you, this truly is a glen of glens. And, as my friends who camp and climb here implore, it needs no more advertisement.

Strathcarron

Nr Bonar Bridge You drive up the N bank of this Highland river from the br outside Ardgay (pron 'Ordguy') which is 3km over the br from Bonar Br. Rd goes 15km to Croick and its remarkable church. The river gurgles and gushes along its rocky course to the Dornoch Firth and there are innumerable places to picnic, swim and stroll further up. Quite heavenly on a warm day.

The Angus Glens

All via Kirriemuir Glen Clova/Glen Prosen/Glen Isla. Isla to W is a woody, approachable glen with a deep gorge, on B954 nr Alyth and the lovely Glenisla Hotel. Others via B955, to Dykehead then rd bifurcates. Both glens stab into the heart of the Grampians. 'Minister's Walk' goes betw them from behind the kirk at Prosen village over the hill to B955 before Clova village (7km). Glen Clova is a walkers' paradise esp from Glendoll 24km from Dykehead; limit of rd. Viewpoint. 'Jock's Rd' to Braemar and the Capel Mounth to Ballater (both 24km). Good hotel at Clova and famous 'Loops of Brandy' walk (2hrs); stark and beautiful.

Glendaruel

Cowal Peninsula The Cowal Peninsula on the A886 betw Colintraive and Strachur. Humble but perfectly formed glen of R Ruel, from Clachan in S (a kirk and an inn) through deciduous meadowland to more rugged grandeur 10km N. Easy walking and cycling. W rd best. Kilmodan carved stones signed. Inver Cottage on L Fyne a gr coffee/food stop.

Glen Lonan

Nr Taynuilt

Betw Taynuilt on A85 and A816 S of Oban. Glen Lonan is another quiet wee glen, but with all the right elements for walking, picnics, cycling and fishing or even just a run in the car. Varying scenery, a bubbling burn (the R Lonan), some standing stones and not many folk. Angus' Garden at the Taynuilt end should not be missed. No marked walks; now get lost!

Glen Trool

Nr Newton Stewart

26km N by A714 via Bargrennan which is on the S Upland Way. A gentle, wooded glen within the vast Galloway Forest Park (Glen Trool is one of the most charming, accessible parts). VC 5km from Bargrennan. Pick up a walk brochure; there are many options. Start of the Merrick climb.

The Sma' Glen

Nr Crieff

Off the A85 to Perth, the A822 to Amulree and Aberfeldy. Sma' meaning small, this is the valley of the R Almond where the Mealls (lumpish, shapeless hills) fall steeply down to the rd. Where the rd turns away from the river, the long-distance path to L Tay begins (28km). Sma' Glen, 8km, has good picnic spots, but they get busy and midgy in summer.

Strathfarrar

Nr Beauly or
Drumnadrochit

Rare unspoiled glen accessed from A831 leaving Drumnadrochit on L Ness via Cannich (30km) or S from Beauly (15km). Signed at Struy. Arrive at gatekeeper's house. Access restricted to 25 cars per day (Cl Tue & till 1.30pm on Wed). For access Oct-Mar 01463 761260; you must be out by 6pm. 22km to head of glen past lochs. Good climbing, walking, fishing. The real peace & quiet!

Falls Of Glomach

25km Kyle of Lochalsh off A87 nr Shiel Br, past Kintail Centre at Morvich then 2km up Glen Croe to br. Walk starts other side; this is most straightforward of several ways. Allow 5/7 hrs for the pilgrimage to one of Britain's highest falls. Path is steep but well trod. Glomach means gloomy and you might feel so, peering into the ravine; from precipice to pool, it's 200m. But to pay tribute, go down carefully to ledge. Vertigo factor and sense of achievement both fairly high. Consult *Where to Walk in Kintail, Glenelg & Lochalsh*, sold locally for the Kintail Mt Rescue Team.

Plodda Falls

Nr Tomich nr Drumnadrochit

A831 from L Ness to Cannich (20km), then 7km to Tomich, a further 5km up mainly woodland track to car park. 200m walk down through woods of Scots Pine and ancient Douglas Fir to one of the most enchanting woodland sites in Britain and the Victorian iron br over the brink of the 150m fall into the churning river below. The dawn chorus here must be amazing. Freezes into winter wonderland (ice climbers from Inverness take advantage). Good hotel in village.

Falls Of Bruar

Nr Blair Atholl

Close to the A9 rd, 12km N of B Atholl. Nr House of Bruar shopping experience so the walk to lower falls is v consumer-led but less crowded than you might expect. The lichen-covered walls of the gorge below the upper falls (1km) are less ogled and more dramatic. Circular path is well marked but steep and rocky in places. Tempting to swim on hot days. ☕

Glenashdale Falls

Arran

5km walk from br on main rd at Whiting Bay. Signed up the burn side, but uphill & further than you think; allow 2hrs (return). Series of falls in a rocky gorge in the woods with paths so you get rt down to the brim & the pools. Swim here, swim in heaven!

Eas Fors

Mull

On the Dervaig to Fionnphort rd 3km from Ulva Ferry; a series of cataracts tumbling down on either side of the rd. Easily accessible. There's a path down the side to the brink where the river plunges into the sea. On a warm day swimming in the sea below the fall is a rare exhilaration.

Skye

Lealt Falls,
Kilt Rock,
Eas Mor

Lealt Falls Impressive torrent of wild mt water about 20km N of Portree on the A855. Walk from nearby car park to grassy ledges & look over or go down to the beach. **Kilt Rock**, a viewpoint much favoured by bus parties, is a few km further (you look over & along the cliffs). Also...

Eas Mor Glen Brittle nr end of rd. 24km from Sligachan. A mt waterfall with the wild Cuillins behind and views to the sea. Start at the Memorial Hut, cross the rd, bear rt, cross burn then follow path uphill.

Eas A' Chual Aluinn

Kylesku

'Britain's highest waterfall' nr the head of Glencoul, is not easy to reach. Kylesku is betw Scourie and Lochinver off the main A894, 20km S of Scourie. There are 2hr cruises at 11am/3pm May-Sept (and 2pm Fri) outside hotel. Falls are a rather distant prospect. The water (allegedly) freefalls for 200m, 4 times further than Niagara.

Steall Falls

Glen Nevis,
Fort William

Take Glen Nevis rd at roundabout outside town centre & drive 'to end' (16km). From the second car park, follow path marked Corrour uphill through woody gorge with R Ness thrashing below. Glen eventually and dramatically opens out. Gr views of the long veils of the Falls. Precarious 3-wire br calls for nerves of steel. Always fun to watch macho types bottle out of doing it! I never have (you can cross further down).

Corrieshalloch Gorge/Falls Of Measach

Nr Ullapool

Jnct of A832 and A835, 20km S of Ullapool; possible to walk down into the gorge from both rds. Most dramatic app is from the car park on the A832 Gairloch rd. Staircase to swing br from whence to consider how such a wee burn could make such a deep gash. V impressive.

The Grey Mare's Tail

Betw Moffat and
Selkirk

About halfway along the wildly scenic A708. 8km from Tibby Shiels Inn, a car park and signs for waterfall. The lower track takes 10/15mins to a viewing place still 500m from falls; the higher, on the other side of the Tail burn, threads betw the austere hills and up to L Skene from which the falls overflow (45/60mins).

The Falls Of Clyde

New Lanark nr
Lanark

Dramatic falls in a long gorge of the Clyde at New Lanark, Robert Owen's 19thC model village. The route gets interesting after the Power Station (1km). There's a 1km climb to the first fall (Cora Linn) & another 1km to the next (Bonnington Linn). Swimming is not advised (but it's gr). For safety, check at VC for details: 01555 665262.

Reekie Linn

Alyth

8km N of town on B951 to Kirriemuir. A picnic site & car park on bend of rd leads by 200m to the wooded gorge of Glen Isla with precipitous viewpoints of defile where Isla is squeezed and falls in tiers for 100ft. Lochside restau nearby.

Falls Of Acharn

Nr Kenmore, Loch Tay

5km along S side of loch on unclass rd. Walk from nr bridge in township of Acharn; falls are signed. Steepish start then 1km up side of gorge; waterfalls on other side. Can be circular route.

Falls Of Rogie

Nr Strathpeffer

Car park on A835 Inverness-Ullapool rd, 10km Strathpeffer. Accessibility makes short walk (250m) quite popular to these hurtling falls on the Blackwater R. Br and salmon ladder (they leap in summer). Woodland trails marked.

Foyers

Loch Ness

On the B862 Ft Augustus to Inverness rd at Foyers village. Park by shops, cross rd, go through fence and down steep track to viewing places (slither-proof shoes advised). R Foyers falls 150m into foaming gorge below and then into L Ness throwing clouds of spray into the trees (you may get drenched).

Falls Of Shin

Nr Lairg, Sutherland

6km E of town on signed rd, car park & falls nearby are easily accessible. Not quite up to the splendours of others on this page, but an excellent place to see salmon battling upstream (best June-Aug). VC with extensive shop. ☕

Loch Lomond

App via the A811 Stirling-Drymen or the A82 Glas-Balloch. Britain's largest inland waterway and a traditional playground with jet-skis, show-off boats. **Lomond Shores** at Balloch is the new, retail gateway to the loch & the **Loch Lomond National Park** which covers a vast area. W bank is most developed: marinas, cruises, ferry to Inchmurrin Island. Rd more picturesque beyond Tarbert to Ardlui; for the non-tourist/real Scots experience, visit the Drover's Inn at Inverarnan. E bank is more natural, wooded, with good walks. Rd winding but picturesque beyond Balmaha towards Ben Lomond.

Loch Ness

One of the best ways to see the loch is on a cruise from Inverness (Jacobite Cruises 01463 233999 1-6 hrs), Drumnadrochit or Fort Augustus. Most tourist traffic uses the main A82 N bank rd converging on Drumnadrochit. On this rd, you can't miss Urquhart Castle. Bu the two best things about L Ness are the S rd (B862) from Ft Augustus back to Inverness; and the detour from Drumnadrochit to Cannich to Glen Affric (20-30km).

Loch Maree

Nr Kinlochewe

A832 betw Kinlochewe and Gairloch. Dotted with islands covered in Scots pine hiding some of the best examples of Viking graves and apparently a money tree in their midst. Easily viewed from the rd which follows its length for 15km. Beinn Eighe rises behind you and the omniscient presence of Slioch is opposite. Aultroy Vistor Centre (5km Kinlochewe), fine walks from car park further on, good accom nr lochside.

Loch An Eilean

Rothiemurchus

An enchanted loch in the heart of the Rothiemurchus Forest. Good VC. You can walk round the loch (5km, allow 1.5hrs). This is classic Highland scenery, a calendar landscape of magnificent Scots pine.

Loch Arkaig

Nr Fort William

An enigmatic loch long renowned for its fishing. From the A82 beyond Spean Br cross the Caledonian Canal, then on by single-track rd through the Clune Forest and the 'Dark Mile' past the 'Witches' Pool' (a cauldron of dark water), to the loch. Bonnie Prince Charlie came this way before and after Culloden; one of his refuge caves is marked on a trail.

Loch Lubhair

Nr Crianlarich

The loch you pass (on the rt) on the A85 to Crianlarich (4km), in Glen Dochart, the upper reaches of the Tay water system. Small and perfect, with bare hills surrounding and fringed with pines and islets. Beautiful scenery that most people just drive past heading for Oban or Ft William.

Loch Achray

Nr Brig o' Turk

The small loch betw **L Katrine** and **L Venachar**. The A821 from Callander skirts both Venachar and Achray (picnic sites). Ben Venue and Ben An rise above: gr walks and views. A one-way forest rd goes round the other side of L Achray thro Achray Forest (enter and leave from the Duke's Pass rd betw Aberfoyle and Brig o' Turk). Details from forest VC 3km N Aberfoyle. Bike hire at L Katrine/ Callander/Aberfoyle: it's the best way to see these lochs.

Glen Finglas Reservoir

Brig O' Turk

A hidden Trossachs gem. It's man-made but a real beauty, surrounded by soft green hills & the odd burn bubbling in. App 'thro' Brig O' Turk houses (past decent caff) and park 2km up road or from new car park 2km before Brig O' Turk from Callander. Walk to right; 5 km walk to head of loch or possible to make the loop round it & back to dam (no path, lots of scrambling; boots only) or go further to Balquhidder – a walk across the heart of Scotland.

Loch Muick

Nr Ballater

At head of rd off B976, the S Dee rd at Ballater. 14km up Glen Muick (pron 'Mick') to car park, VC and 100m to loch side. Lochnagar rises above and walk also begins here for Capel Mount and Glen Clova. 3hr walk around loch and any number of ambles. The lodge where Vic met John is at the furthest pt (well it would be). Open aspect with grazing deer and not too much forestry.

Loch Eriboll

North Coast

90km W of Thurso. The long sea loch that indents into the coast for 15km and which you drive round on the main A838. Deepest natural anchorage in the UK, with every aspect of loch side scenery including, alas, fish cages. Ben Hope nr the head of the loch with a perfect beach (my own private Idaho) on the coast.

Loch Trool

Nr Newton Stewart

The small, celebrated loch in a bowl of the Galloway Hills reached via Bargrennan 14km N via A714 and 8km to end of rd. Woodland VC/café on the way.

Good walks but best viewed from Bruce's Stone and the slopes of Merrick. Idyllic.

Loch Morar

Nr Mallaig

70km W of Ft William by the A850 (wildly scenic & much improved). Morar village is 6km from Mallaig & a single track rd leads away from the coast to the loch (only 500m but out of sight) then along it for 5km to Bracora. It's the prettiest part with wooded islets, small beaches, loch side meadows & bobbing boats. The rd stops at a turning place but a track continues from Bracorina to Tarbet & it's possible to connect with a post boat & sail back to Mallaig on L Nevis around 3.30pm (check TIC). L Morar, joined to the coast by the shortest river in Britain, also has the deepest water. There is a spookiness about it and just possibly a monster called Morag.

Loch Tummel

Nr Pitlochry

W from Pitlochry on B8019 to Rannoch (and the end of the rd), L Tummel comes into view, as it did for Queen Victoria, scintillating beneath you, and on a clear day with Schiehallion beyond. This N side has good walks, but the S rd from Faskally just outside Pitlochry is the one to take to get down to the lochside to picnic etc.

Loch Lundavra

Nr Fort William

Here's a secret loch in the hills, but not far from the well-trodden tracks through the glens and the sunny streets of Ft William. Go up Lundavra Rd from roundabout at W end of main st, out of town, over cattle grid and on (to end of rd) 8km. You should have it to yourself; good picnic spots and gr view of Ben Nevis. W Highland Way comes this way.

Ardnamurchan

For anyone who loves trees (or hills, gr coastal scenery & raw nature), this far-flung peninsula is a revelation. App from S via Corran ferry on A82 S of Ft William or N from Lochailort on A830 Mallaig–Ft William rd or from Mull. Many marked & unmarked trails but consult TIC & local literature. To visit Ardnamurchan is to fall in love with Scotland again. Woods esp around L Sunart.

Randolph's Leap

Nr Forres

Spectacular gorge of the plucky little Findhorn lined with beautiful beechwoods and a gr place to swim or picnic, so listen up. Go either: 10km S of Forres on the A940 for Grantown, then the B9007 for Ferness and Carrbridge. 1km from the sign for Logie Steading and 500m from the narrow stone br, there's a pull-over place on the bend. The woods are on the other side of the rd. Or: take the A939 S from Nairn or N from Grantown and at Ferness take the B9007 for Forres. Approaching from this direction, it's about 6km along the rd; the pull-over is on your rt. If you come to Logie Steading in this direction you've missed it; don't – you will miss one of the sylvan secrets of the N.

Lochaweside

2-8KM CIRC
XBIKE 2-A-2

Unclassified rd on N side of loch betw Kilchrenan and Ford, centred on Dalavich. Brochure from local hotels around Kilchrenan and Dalavich PO, describes 6 walks in the mixed, mature forest all starting from car-parking places on the rd. 3 from the Barnaline car park are trail-marked and could be followed without brochure. Avich Falls route crosses R Avich

after 2km with falls on return route.
Inverinan Glen is always nice. 'Timber trail'
from The Big Tree/Cruachan car park 2km
S of Dalavich takes in the loch, a waterfall
& is easy on the eye & foot (4km). The
track from the car park N of Kilchrenan on
the B845 back to Taynuilt isn't on the brochure, may be less travelled and also fine.

Puck's Glen

Nr Dunoon

3KM CIRC XBIKE
1-A-1

Close to the gates of the Younger Botanic
Garden at Benmore on the other side of
the A815 to Stracher 12km N of Dunoon.
A short, exhilarating woodland walk from
a convenient car park. Ascend thro' trees
then down into a faery glen, foll the burn
back to the rd. Some swimming pools.

Rothiemurchus Forest

✓

Nr Aviemore

The place to experience the magic and the
majesty of the gr Caledonian Forest and
the beauty of Scots pine. App from B970,
the rd that parallels the A9 from
Coylumbridge to Kincraig/Kingussie. 2km
from Inverdruie nr Coylumbridge follow
sign for L an Eilean; one of the most
perfect lochans in these or any woods.
Loch circuit 5km. Good free brochure for
all forest activities from TICs.

Ariundle Oakwoods

Strontian

5KM CIRC mtBIKE
1-A-2

35km Ft William via Corran Ferry. Walk
guide brochure at Strontian TIC. Many
walks around L Sunart and Ariundle: rare
oak and other native species. You see how
v different Scotland's landscape was
before the Industrial Revolution used up
the wood. Start over town br, turning rt for
Polloch. Go on past Ariundle Centre, with
good home-baking café and park. 2 walks;
well marked.

Balmacarra, Lochalsh Woodland Garden

Nr Kyle of Lochalsh

CIRC XBIKE 1-A-1

5km S Kyle of Lochalsh on A87. A woodland walk around the shore of L Alsh, centred on Lochalsh House. Mixed woodland in fairly formal gdn setting where you are confined to paths. Views to Skye. A fragrant & verdant amble. Ranger service.

The Birks O' Aberfeldy

3KM CIRC XBIKE 1-A-2

Circular walk through oak, beech and the birch (or birk) woods of the title, easily reached and signed from town main st (1km). Steep-sided wooded glen of the Moness Burn with attractive falls esp the higher one spanned by br where the 2 marked walks converge. This is where Burns 'spread the lightsome days' in his eponymous poem. Nice tearm in town.

The Hermitage Dunkeld

2KM CIRC XBIKE 1-A-1

On A9 2km N of Dunkeld. Popular, easy, accessible walks along glen and gorge of R Braan with pavilion o/look the Falls and, further on, 'Ossian's Cave'. Also uphill Craig Vean walks starts here to good view pt (2km). Several woody walks around Dunkeld/Birnam; gd leaflet from TIC. 2km along river is **Rumbling Bridge**, a deep gorge, & beyond it gr spots for swimming.

Glenmore Forest Park

Nr Aviemore

Along from Coylumbridge (and adj Rothiemurchus) on rd to ski resort, the forest trail area centred on L Morlich (sandy beaches, good swimming, water sports). Visitor centre has maps of walk and bike trails and an activity programme.

Above The Pass Of Leny

Callendar

2 OR 4KM   CIRC
XBIKE 1-A-1

A walk through mixed forest (beech, oak, birch, pine) with gr Trossachs views. Start from main car park on A84 4km N of Callander (the Falls of Leny are on opp side of rd, 100m away) on path at back, to the left – path parallels rd at first (don't head straight up). Way-marked & boarded where marshy, the path divides after 1km to head further up to crest (4km return) or back down (2km). Another glorious walk is to the **Bracklinn falls** – signed off E end of Callander Main St; start by golf course (1km). Also loop to the Craggs (adds 2km).

Loch Tummel Walks

Nr Pitlochry

Mixed woodland N of L Tummel reached by the B8019 from Pitlochry to Rannoch. Visitor centre at Queen's View & walks in the Allean Forest which take in some historical sites (a restored farmstead, standing stones) start nearby (2-4km). There are many other walks in area and the Forest Enterprise brochure is worth following (available from VC and local TICs).

The New Galloway Forest

Huge area of forest & hill country with every type of trail incl part of S Upland Way from Bargrennan to Dalry. VCs at Kirroughtree (5km Newton Stewart) & Clatteringshaws L on the 'Queen's Way' (9km New Galloway). Glen & L Trool are v fine; the 'Retreat Oakwood' nr Laurieston has 5km trails. Kitty's in New Galloway has great cakes & tea. There's a river pool on the Raiders' Rd. One could ramble on... Get the TIC brochure.

Glencoe

The A82 from Crianlarich to Ballachulish is a fine drive, but from the extraterrestrial L Ba onwards, there can be few rds anywhere that have direct contact with such imposing scenery. After Kingshouse and Buachaille Etive Mor on the left, the mts and ridges rising on either side of Glencoe proper are truly awesome. The new VC, more discreet than the former nr Glencoe village, sets the topographical and historical scene.

Shiel Bridge-Glenelg

The switchback rd that climbs from the A87 (Ft William 96km) at Shiel Br over the 'hill' and down to the coast opposite the Sleat Peninsula in Skye (short ferry to Kylerhea). As you climb you're almost as high as the surrounding summits and there's the classic view across L Duich to the 5 Sisters of Kintail. Coming back you think you're going straight into the loch! It's really worth driving to Glenelg and beyond to Arnisdale & ethereal L Hourn (16km).

Applecross

120km Inverness. From Tornapress nr Lochcarron for 18km. Leaving the A896 seems like leaving civilisation; the winding ribbon heads into monstrous mts and the high plateau at the top is another planet. It's not for the faint-hearted and Applecross is a relief to see with its campsite/coffee shop and a far-away inn: the legendary Applecross Inn. This hair-raising rd rises 2000' in 6 mls. See how they built it at the Applecross Heritage Centre.

Glen Torridon

The A896 which follows the glen to Kinlochewe. Starting in delightful Diabeg allows views of staggering Ben Alligin, but either side of L Torridon is impressive. Excl hotel. Towards Kinlochewe there's Liatach & Beinn Elghe. Much to climb, much to merely amaze.

Rothesay-Tighnabruaich

A886/A8003. The most celebrated part of this route is the latter, the A8003 down by L Riddon to Tighnabruaich along the hill sides which give the breathtaking views of Bute & the Kyles, but the all of it, with its diverse aspects of lochside, riverine and rocky scenery, is supernatural. Includes short crossing betw Rhubodach and Colintraive. Gr hotel/retau - **The Royal** - at Tighnabruaich.

The Golden Road

South Harris

The main rd in Harris follows the W coast, notable for bays & beaches. This is the other one, winding round a series of coves and inlets with offshore skerries & a treeless rocky hinterland – classic Hebridean landscape, esp Finsbay. Good caff in the middle - **The Skoon Art Café**. Tweed is woven in this area; you can visit the crofts where you can buy some.

Lochinver-Drumbeg-Kylestrome

The coast rd N from Lochinver (35km) is marvellous; essential Assynt. Actually best travelled N-S so that you leave the splendid vista of Eddrachilles Bay and pass through lochan, moor and even woodland, touching the coast again by sandy beaches (at Stoer a rd leads 7km to the lighthouse and the walk to the Old Man of Storr) and app Lochinver (possible detour to Auchmelvich and beaches) with one of the classic long views of Suilven. Excl caff at Drumbeg half-way round: **Drumbeg Designs & Little Tea Garden**. Open 7 days, Easter-Oct till 4.45pm.

Lochinver-Achiltibuie

Nr Ullapool

And S from Lochinver Achiltibuie is 40km from Ullapool; so this is the route from the N; 28km of winding rd/unwinding Highland scenery; through glens, mts and silver sea. Known locally as the 'wee mad rd' (it is maddening if you're in a hurry). Passes **Achin's Bookshop and Café**, the path to Kirkaig Falls and the mighty Suilven.

Sleat Peninsula

Skye

The unclassified rd off the A851 (main Sleat rd) esp coming from S, i.e. take rd at Ostaig nr Gaelic College (gr place to stay nearby); it meets coast after 9km. Affords rare views of the Cuillins from a craggy coast. Returning to 'main' rd S of Isleornsay, pop into the gr hotel pub there.

Leaderfoot-Clintmains

Nr St Boswells

The B6356 betw the A68 (look out for Leaderfoot viaduct & signs for Dryburgh) & the B6404 Kelso-St Boswells rd. This small rd, busy in summer, links Scott's View and Dryburgh Abbey (find by following Abbey signs) and Smailholm Tower, and passes through classic Border/ Tweedside scenery. Don't miss Irvine's View if you want to see the Borders. Nice GH - **Clint Lodge**.

Braemar-Linn Of Dee

12km of renowned Highland river scenery along the upper valley of the (Royal) Dee. The Linn (rapids) is at the end of the rd, but there are river walks and the start of the gr Glen Tilt walk to Blair Atholl. Deer abound.

Ballater-Tomintoul

The ski road to the Lecht, the A939 which leaves the Royal Deeside rd (A93) W of Ballater before it gets really royal. A ribbon of road in the bare Grampians, past the sentinel ruin Corgarff (open to view, 250m walk; extensive repairs '05) & the valley of the trickling Don. Rd proceeds seriously uphill & main viewpoints are S of the Lecht. There is just nobody for miles. Walks in Glenlivet estates S of Tomintoul.

Fort Augustus-Dores

Nr Inverness

The B862 often single-track rd that follows and latterly skirts L Ness. Quieter & more interesting than the main W bank A82. Starts in rugged country & follows the straight rd built by Wade to tame the Highlands. Reaches the lochside at Foyers & goes all the way to Dores (15km from Inverness). Paths to the shore of the loch. Fabulous untrodden woodlands nr Errogie (marked) & the spooky graveyard adj Boleskin House where Aleister Crowley did his dark magic and Jimmy Page of Led Zeppelin may have done his. 35km total; worth taking slowly.

The Duke's Pass

Aberfoyle-Brig O' Turk

Of the many rds through the Trossachs, this one is spectacular though gets busy; many possibilities for stopping, exploration & gr views. Good viewpoint 4km from L Achray Hotel, above rd & lay-by. One-way forest rd goes round L Achray. Good hill walking starts & L Katrine Ferry (2km) 4/5 times a day Apr-Oct (01877 376316). Bike hire at L Katrine, Aberfoyle & Callander.

Glenfinnan-Mallaig

The Road to the Isles

The A830 runs through some of the most impressive and romantic landscapes in the Highlands, splendid in any weather (it does rain rather a lot), to the coast at the Sands of Morar. This is deepest Bonnie Prince Charlie country and demonstrates what a misty eye he had for magnificent settings. A full-throttle bikers' dream. The rd is shadowed for much of the way by the West Highland Railway, which is an even better way to enjoy the scenery. Rd recently improved, esp Arisaig–Mallaig.

Lochailort-Acharacle

Off from the A830 above at Lochailort and turning S on the A861, the coastal section of this gr scenery is superb esp in the setting sun, or in May when the rhodies are out. Glen Uig Inn is rough & ready! This is the rd to the Castle Tioram shoreline (don't miss it) & glorious Ardnamurchan.

Knapdale

Lochgilphead-Tarbert, Argyll

B8024 off the main A83 follows the coast for most of its route. Views to Jura are immense. In the middle in exactly the right place is a superb inn/gastropub, the **Kilberry Inn**. Take it easy on this v Scottish 35kms of single track.

Amulree-Kenmore

Unclassified single-track & v narrow rd from the hill-country hamlet of Amulree to cosy Kenmore signed Glen Quaich. Past L Freuchie, a steep climb takes you to a plateau ringed by magnificent (far) mts to L Tay. Steep descent to L Tay and Kenmore. Don't forget to close the gates.

Pure Perthshire

Muthill-Comrie

A route which takes you thro some of the best scenery in central Scotland & ends up (best this way round) in Comrie with teashops & other pleasures. Leave Muthill by Crieff rd turning left (2km) into Drummond Castle grounds up a glorious avenue of beech trees (gate open 2-5pm). Visit gdn; continue through estate. At gate, go rt, following signs for Strowan. V quiet rd; we have it to ourselves. First jnct, go left following signs (4km). At T-jnct, go left to Comrie (7km). Best have a map, but if not, who cares – it's all bonny!

The Heads Of Ayr

The coast rd S from Ayr to Culzean & Turnberry incl these headlands, gr views of Ailsa Craig & Arran & some horrible caravan parks. The Electric Brae S of Dunure vill is famously worth stopping on (your car runs the opposite way to the slope). Culzean grounds are gorgeous.

The Quirang

Skye

Best app is from Uig direction taking the rt-hand unclassified rd off the hairpin of the A855 above and 2km from town (more usual app from Staffin side is less of a revelation). View (and walk) from car park, the massive rock formations of a towering, contorted ridge. Solidified lava heaved and eroded into fantastic pinnacles. Fine views also across Staffin Bay to Wester Ross.

An Teallach and Liathach

An Teallach, that gr favourite of Scottish hill walkers (40km S of Ullapool by the A835/A832), is best viewed from the side of Little L Broom or the A832 just before you get to Dundonald.

The classic view of the other great Torridon mts (**Beinn Eighe**, pron 'Ben A', & **Liathach** together, 100km S by rd from Ullapool) in Glen Torridon 4km from Kinlochewe. This viewpt is not marked but it's on the track around L Clair which is reached from the entrance to the Coulin estate off the A896, Glen Torridon rd (be aware of stalking). Park outside gate; no cars allowed, 1km walk to lochside. These mts have to be seen to be believed.

From Raasay

There are several fabulous views looking over to Skye from Raasay, the small island reached by ferry from Sconser. The panorama from Dun Caan, the hill in the centre of the island (444m) is of Munro proportions, producing an elation incommensurate with the small effort required to get there. Start from the rd to the 'N End' or ask at the Activity Centre in the big house: the Dolphin Café (& bar).

The Summer Isles

Achiltibuie

The Summer Isles are a scattering of islands seen from the coast of Achiltibuie (and the lounge of the Summer Isles Hotel) and visited by boat from Ullapool. But the best place to see them, and the stunning perspective of this western shore is on the road to Altandhu, possibly to the pub there. On way to Achiltibuie, turn rt thro Polbain, thro' Allandhu, then on 500m past turning for Reiff. There's a bench. Sit on it. You're alive! And further on, 500m round the corner, the distant mts of Assynt all in a row.

The Rest And Be Thankful

On A83 L Lomond-Inveraray rd where it's met by the B828 from Lochgoilhead. In summer the rest may be from driving stress and you may not be thankful for the camera-toting masses, but this was always one of the most accessible, rewarding viewpoints in the land. Surprisingly, none of the encompassing hills are Munros but they are nonetheless dramatic. Only a few carpets of conifer to smother the grandeur of the crags as you look down the valley.

Elgol

Skye

End of the rd, the B8083, 22km from Broadford. The classic view of the Cuillins from across L Scavaig and of Soay & Rum. Cruises (Apr-Oct) in the *Bella Jane* (0800 731 3089) or *The Misty Isle* (May-Sept, not Sun 01471 866288) to the famous corrie of L Coruisk, painted by Turner, romanticised by Walter Scott. A journey you'll remember.

Camas Nan Geall

Ardnamurchan

12km Salen on B8007. 4km from Ardnamurchan's Natural History Centre 65km Ft William. Coming esp from the Kilchoan direction, a magnificent bay appears below you, where the rd first meets the sea. Almost symmetrical with high cliffs and a perfect field (still cultivated) in the bowl fringed by a shingle beach. Car park viewpoint and there is a path down. Amazing Ardnamurchan!

Glengarry

3km after Tomdoun t/off on A87, Invergarry-Kyle of Lochalsh rd. Lay-by with viewfinder. An uncluttered vista up and down loch and glen with not a house in sight (pity about the salmon cages). Distant peaks of Knoydart are identified, but not L Quoich nestling spookily and full of fish in the wilderness at the head of the glen. Gaelic mouthfuls of mts on the orientation board. Bonnie Prince Charlie passed this way.

Scott's View

St Boswells

Off A68 at Leaderfoot Br nr St Boswells, signed Gattonside. 'The View', old Walter's favourite (the horses still stopped there long after he'd gone), is 4km along the rd (Dryburgh Abbey 3km further). Magnificent sweep of his beloved Border country, but only in one direction. If you cross the rd & go through the kissing gate and head up the hill towards the jagged standing stone that comes into view, you reach ...

Irvine's View

The full panorama from the Cheviots to the Lammermuirs. This, the finest view in southern Scotland, is only a furlong further (than Scott's View, above) – cross rd from layby, go thro' kissing gate & climb thro' rough pasture; mind the livestock. On first rise, you'll see the spiky standing stone – head for it; about 15 mins' walk). This is where I'd like my bench – but some bastard has erected a horrible phone mast up there (not that I go anywhere without a moby myself). Turn your back on it & gaze into the beautiful Borders.

Penielheugh

Nr Ancrum

An obelisk visible for miles, on a rise which offers some of the most exhilarating views of the Borders. Also known as the Waterloo Monument, it was built on the Marquis of Lothian's estate to commemorate the battle. It's said that the woodland on the surrounding slopes represents the positions of Wellington's troops. From A68 opposite Ancrum t/off, on B6400, go 1km past Monteviot Gardens up steep, unmarked rd to left (cycle sign) for 150m; sign says 'Vehicles Prohibited, etc'. Park, walk up through woods.

The Law

Dundee

Few cities have such a single good viewpoint. To N of the centre, it reveals the panoramic perspective of the city on the estuary of the silvery Tay. Best to walk from town; the one-way system is a nightmare, tho there are signposts.

Queen's View

Loch Tummel nr Pitlochry

8km on B8019 to Kinloch Rannoch. Car park and 100m walk to rocky knoll where pioneers of tourism, Queen Victoria & Prince Albert, were 'transported into ecstasies' by view of L Tummel & Schiehallion. Their view was flooded by a hydro scheme after WW2; more recently it has spawned a whole view-driven visitor experience (& it costs a quid to park). It all... makes you wonder.

The Rallying Place Of The Maclarens

Balquhidder

Short climb from behind the church, signed Creag an Tuire, steep at first. Superb view down L Voil, the Balquhidder Braes and the real Rob Roy Country & gr caff with home-baking on your descent.

Califer

Nr Forres

7km from Forres on A96 to Elgin, turn rt for 'Pluscarden', follow rd for 5km. Viewpoint is on rd & looks down across Findhorn Bay & the wide vista of the Moray Firth to the Black Isle & Ben Wyvis. Fantastic light.

The Malcolm Memorial

Langholm

3km from Langholm and signed from main A7, a single-track rd leads to a path to this obelisk raised to celebrate the military and masonic achievements of one John Malcolm. The eulogy is fulsome esp compared with that for Hugh MacDiarmid on the cairn by the stunning sculpture at the start of the path. Views from the obelisk, however, are among the finest in the S, encompassing a vista from the Lakeland Fells and the Solway Firth to the wild Border hills. Path 1km.

Duncryne Hill

Gartocharn nr Balloch

Gartocharn is betw Balloch and Drymen on the A811, and this view, was recommended by writer and outdoorsman Tom Weir as 'the finest viewpoint of any small hill in Scotland'. Turn up Duncryne rd at the E end of village and park 1km on left by a small wood (a sign reads 'Woods reserved for Teddy bears'). The hill is only 470ft high and 'easy', but the view of L Lomond and the Kilpatrick Hills is superb.

Blackhill

Lesmahagow nr Glasgow

28km S of city. Another marvellous outlook, but in the opposite direction from above. Take jnct 10/11 on M74, then off the B7078 signed Lanark, take the B7018. 4km along past Clarkston Farm, head uphill for 1km & park by Water Board mound. Walk uphill through fields to rt for about 1km. Unprepossessing hill which unexpectedly reveals a vast vista of most of E central Scotland (& most of the uphill is in the car).

Tongue

From the causeway across the kyle, or better, follow the minor rd to Talmine on the W side, look S to Ben Loyal or north to the small islands off the coast.

Cairnpapple Hill

Nr Linlithgow

Volcanic geology, neolithic henge, E Scottish agriculture, the Forth plain, the Bridges, Grangemouth industrial complex & telecoms masts: not all pretty, but the whole of Scotland at a glance. App from the 'Beecraigs' rd off W end of Linlithgow main st. Go past the Beecraigs t/off and continue for 3km. Cairnpapple is signed.

Stirling Castle

*Historic Scotland.
Standard hrs are:
Apr-end Sept
Mon-Sat
9.30am-6.30pm;
Sun 2-6.30pm.
Oct-Mar Mon-Sat
9.30am-4.30pm;
Sun 2-4.30pm.*

Dominating the town and the plain, this like Edin Castle is worth the hype and the history. Although built for warfare, it does seem a v civilised billet, with peaceful gdns and rampart walks from which the views are excellent. Incls the Renaissance Palace of James V and the Great Hall of James IV restored to full magnificence. The Costa caff is a bit of a letdown in these historical circumstances (but it does hot food).

Edinburgh Castle

*Historic Scotland.
For standard
opening hrs see
Stirling Castle
details.*

City centre. Impressive from any angle and all the more so from inside. Despite the tides of tourists and time, it still enthralls. Superb perspectives of the city and of Scottish history. Stone of Destiny & the Crown Jewels are the Big Attractions. Café and restau (superb views) with efficient, but uninspiring catering operation; open only castle hrs and to castle visitors.

Brodie Castle

Nr Nairn

*National Trust for
Scotland.
Mar-Sept 12-4pm
(cl Fri/Sat May,
June, Sept); Sun
1.30-5.30pm.
W/ends in Oct.*

6-7km W of Forres off main A96. More a (Z-plan) tower house than a castle, dating from 1567. With a minimum of historical hocum, this 16/17thC, but mainly Victorian, country house is furnished from rugs to moulded ceilings in the most excellent taste. Every picture (v few gloomies) bears examination. The nursery and nanny's rm, the guest rms, indeed all the rms, are eminently habitable. I could live in the library. There are regular musical evenings and other events (01309 641371 for event programme). Tearoom and informal walks in grounds. An avenue leads to a lake; in spring the daffodils are famous. Grounds open AYR till sunset.

Culzean Castle

Maybole

National Trust for Scotland.
Apr-Oct 11am-5.30pm.

24km S of Ayr on A719. Impossible to convey the scale and the scope of the house and country park. From the 12thC, but rebuilt by Robert Adam in 1775, its grandeur is almost out of place in this exposed cliff-top position. 560 acres of grounds including cliff-top walk, formal gdns, walled gdn, Swan Pond and Happy Valley. Many special 'events'. Culzean is pron 'Cullane'. And you can stay.

Falkland Palace

Falkland

National Trust for Scotland.
Mar-Oct 10-6pm.
Sun 1-5.30pm.

Middle of farming Fife, 15km from M90 jnct 8. Not a castle at all, but the hunting palace of the Stewart dynasty. Despite its recreational rather than political role, it's one of the landmark buildings in Scottish history and in the 16thC was the finest Renaissance building in Britain. They all came here for archery, falconry and hunting boar and deer on the Lomonds; and for Royal Tennis which is displayed and explained. The house is dark and rich and redolent of those days of 'dancin and deray at Falkland on the Grene'. Plant shop & events programme.

Castle Of Mey

Nr Thurso

May-July, mid Aug-Sept but check (01847 851473). Cl Fri.

Actually nr John o' Groats (off A836), castles don't get further-flung than this. Stunted trees, frequent wind & a wild coast but the Queen Mother famously fell in love with this dilapidated house in 1952, filled it with things she found & was given & turned it into one of the most human & endearing of the Royal (if not all aristocratic) residences. Guides in every rm tell the story & if you didn't love her already, you will when you leave. Charles & Camilla still visit.

Cawdor Castle

Cawdor nr Nairn & Inverness

May-early Oct, 7 days, 10am-5.30pm.

The mighty Cawdor of Macbeth fame. Most of the family clear off for the summer and leave their romantic yet habitable & yes... stylish castle, sylvan grounds and gurgling Cawdor Burn to you. An easy drive (25km) to Brodie (above) means you can see 2 of Scotland's most appealing castles in one day. Gdns are gorgeous. 9-hole golf.

Blair Castle

Blair Atholl

Mar-Oct 9.30am-4.30pm (last adm) daily.

Impressive from the A9, the castle and landscape of the Dukes of Atholl (present duke not present); 10km N of Pitlochry. Hugely popular; almost a holiday camp atmos. Numbered rms chock-full of 'collections': costumes, toys, weapons, stag skulls – so many things! Upstairs, the more usual stuffed apartments including the Jacobite bits. Walk in the policies.

Glamis

Forfar

Easter-mid Oct, 10.30am. Last admn 4.45pm.

8km from Forfar via A94 or off main A929, Dundee-Aber rd (t/off 10km N of Dundee, a picturesque app). Fairy-tale castle in majestic setting. Seat of the Strathmore family (Queen Mum spent her childhood here) for 600 yrs; every rm an example of the interior of a certain period. Guided tours (continuous, 50mins duration). Restau/gallery shop haven for tourists (& for an excl bridie). Italian Gdns & nature trail well worth 500m walk.

Brodick Castle

Arran

4km from town (bike hire 01770 302868). Impressive, well-maintained castle, gdns and grounds. Goat Fell in the background and the sea through the trees. Dating

National Trust for Scotland. Easter-Oct daily until 4pm (last adm).

from 13thC and until the 1950s the home of the Dukes of Hamilton. An over-antlered hall leads to liveable rms with portraits and heirlooms, an atmos of long-ago afternoons. Tangible sense of relief in the kitchens now all the entertaining is over. Marvellous grounds open AYR.

Duart Castle

Mull

April Sun-Thur 11-4pm. May-Oct 10.30am-5.30pm.

13thC ancestral seat of the Clan Maclean & home to Sir Lachlan & Lady Maclean. With walls as thick as a truck and the sheer isolation of the place, any prospect of attack must have seemed doomed from the outset. Now happier and homlier, the only attacking that gets done these days is on scones in the superior tearoom. ☕

Torosay Castle

Mull

Mar-Oct 10.30am-5pm.

3km from Craignure and the ferry. A Victorian *arriviste* in this strategic corner where Duart Castle has ruled for centuries. Not many apartments open but who could blame them – this is a family home, endearing and eccentric. There's a human proportion to the house and its contents which is rare in such places. The gdns, attributed to Lorimer, are fabulous, and open AYR 9am-7pm.

Dunvegan Castle

Skye

Mar-Oct 10am-5.30pm, wint 11-4pm.

3km Dunvegan village. Romantic history and setting, though more baronial than castellate, the result of a mid-19thC restoration that incorporated the disparate parts. Necessary crowd management leads you through a series of rms where the Fairy Flag has pride of place. Lovely gdns down to the loch. Busy café and gift shop.

Eilean Donan

Dornie

Mar-Nov,
10-5.30pm.

On A87, 13km before Kyle of Lochalsh. A calendar favourite. Inside, a decent slice of history for the price. The Banqueting Hall with its Pipers' Gallery must make for splendid dinner parties for the Macraes. Much military regalia amongst the bric-a-brac, but also the impressive Raasay Punchbowl partaken of by Johnson and Boswell. Mystical views from ramparts.

Castle Menzies

Nr Aberfeldy

Apr-Oct
10.30am-5pm,
Sun 2-5pm.

On B846, 7km W of Aberfeldy. The 16thC stronghold of the Menzies (pron 'Ming-iss'), one of Scotland's oldest clans. Sparsely furnished with odd clan memorabilia, the house conveys more of a sense of Jacobite times than many more brimful of bric-a-brac. Bonnie Prince Charlie stopped here on the way to Culloden. Open farmland situation, so manured rather than manicured grounds.

Scone Palace

Nr Perth

Easter-Oct 7days
9.30am-4.45pm
(last adm.) Fri
only in wint
10am-5pm.

On A93 rd to Blairgowrie and Braemar. A 'great house', home to the Earl of Mansfield, and gorgeous grounds. Famous for the 'Stone of Scone' on which the Kings of Scots were crowned, and the Queen Vic bedroom. Maze and pinetum. Many contented animals greet you.

Kellie Castle

Nr Pittenweem

May-Sept 1-5pm.

Major castle in Fife. Dating from 14thC and restored by Robert Lorimer, his influence evidenced by magnificent plaster ceilings and furniture. The gdns, nursery and kitchen recall all the old Victorian virtues. The old-fashioned roses still bloom for us. Grounds open AYR.

Craigievar

Nr Banchory

National Trust for Scotland.
Apr-Sept, Fri-Tues only 12-5.30pm (last adm 4.45pm).

15km N of main A93 Aber-Braemar rd betw Banchory and Aboyne. A classic tower house, perfect like a porcelain miniature. Random windows, turrets, balustrades. Limited access (only 8 people at a time) means you are spared the shuffling hordes, but don't go unless you are respecter of the NTS conservation policy.

Drum Castle

Nr Aberdeen

National Trust for Scotland.
Easter-Sept 12.30-5.30 (from 10am June-Aug).

1km off main A93 Aberdeen-Braemar rd betw Banchory and Peterculter. Gifted to one William De Irwin by Robert the Bruce, it combines the original keep, a Jacobean mansion and Victorian expansionism. Grounds have a peaceful & exceptional walled rose gdn (Apr-Sept 10-6pm). Tower can be climbed for gr views. I thought the Old Wood of Drum was a bit of a swizz ie not old at all.

Balmoral

Nr Ballater

Daily 10-5pm, Easter-July.

On A93 betw Ballater and Braemar. Limited access to the house so grounds (open Apr-July) are more rewarding. For royalty rooters only, and if you like Landseers ... Crathie Church is along the main rd but services have never been quite the same Sunday attraction since Di and Fergie on a prince's arm.

Dunrobin Castle

Golspie

Apr-mid Oct. Check 01408 633177 for times.

Home of the Dukes of Sutherland and the biggest house in the Highlands. The first Duke infamously started the Clearances. The family transformed the castle into a *château*, filling it with their obscene wealth; but now that conspicuous consumption is just history. The gdns are still fabulous.

The American Monument

Islay

On Islay's SW peninsula, known as the Oa (pron 'Oh'), 13km from Pt Ellen. A monument to commemorate the shipwrecks nearby of 2 American ships, the *Tuscania* & the *Ontranto*; both sank in 1918 at the end of the war. The obelisk o/look this sea – which is often beset by storms – from a spectacular headland, the sort of disquieting place where you could imagine looking round & finding the person you're with has disappeared. Take rd from Pt Ellen past Maltings marked Mull of Oa 12km, thro gate and left at broken sign. Park & walk 1.5km steadily uphill to monument.

Wallace Monument

Stirling

Open daily AYR. 01786 472140 for details; hrs vary.

Visible for miles and with gr views, though not as dramatic as Stirling Castle. App from A91 or Br of Allan rd. 150m walk from car park and 246 steps up. Victorian gothic spire marks the place where Scotland's gr patriot swooped down upon the English at the Battle of Stirling Br. Mel Gibson's *Braveheart* increased visitors though his face on the Wallace statue is thanks too far. In the 'Hall of Heroes' the new heroines section requires a feminist leap of the imagination. The famous sword is v big.

The Grave Of Flora Macdonald

Skye

Kilmuir on A855, Uig-Staffin rd, 40km N of Portree. A 10ft-high Celtic cross supported against the wind, high on the ridge o/look the Uists from whence she came. Long after the legendary journey, her funeral in 1790 attracted the biggest crowd since Culloden. The present memorial replaced the original, which was chipped away by souvenir hunters.

Carfin Grotto

Motherwell
Open at all times.

Between Motherwell & the M8, take the B road into Carfin and it's by Newarthill Rd. Gardens & pathways with shrines, pavilion, chapel & memorials. Latest statues: St Peregrine (patron saint of cancer sufferers) & one for the Lockerbie victims. A major Catholic centre and never less than thought-provoking as the rest of us go station to station. Carfin Pilgrimage Centre adj open daily, 10am-5pm AYR.

Hamilton Mausoleum

Strathclyde Park

Off (and visible from) M74 at jnct 5/6, 15km from Glas. Huge, over-the-top/over-the-tomb (though removed 1921) stone memorial to the 10th Duke of Hamilton. Guided tours Wed/Sat/Sun 3pm in summer, 2pm in wint. Eerie and chilling and with remarkable acoustics – the 'longest echo in Europe'. Give it a shout or take your violin. Information and tickets from Hamilton Museum: 01698 328232.

Peniel Heugh

Nr Ancrum/
Jedburgh

(Pron 'Pinal-hue'.) An obelisk visible for miles and on a rise which offers some of the most exhilarating views of the Borders. Also known as the Waterloo Monument, it was built on the Marquis of Lothian's estate to commemorate the battle. It's said that the woodland on the surrounding slopes represents the positions of Wellington's troops. From A68 opposite Ancrum t/off, on B6400, go 1km past Monteviot Gardens up steep, unmarked rd to left (cycle sign) for 150m; sign says 'Vehicles Prohibited, etc'. Park, walk up through woods.

The Hopetoun Monument

Athelstaneford nr Haddington

The needle atop a rare rise in E Lothian (Byres Hill) and a gr vantage point from which to view the county from the Forth to the Lammermuirs and Edinburgh over there. Off A6737 Haddington to Aberlady rd on B1343 to Athelstaneford. Car park and short climb. Tower usually open and viewfinder boards at top but take a torch; it's a dark climb. Good gentle 'ridge' walk E from here.

The Pineapple

Airth

From Airth N of Grangemouth, take A905 to Stirling & after 1km the B9124 for Cowie. It sits on the edge of a walled gdn at the end of the drive. 45ft high, it was built in 1761 as a gdn retreat by an unknown architect & remained 'undiscovered' until 1963. How exotic the fruit must have seemed in the 18thC, never mind this extraordinary folly. Grounds open AYR; oddly enough, you can stay here (2 bedrms, 01628 825925).

John Lennon Memorial

Durness

In garden created 2002 (a BBC Beechgrove project) amazing in itself surviving these harsh, v northern conditions, an inscribed slate memorial to JL who for many yrs as a child came here with his aunt for the hols. 'There are places I'll remember all my life' from *Rubber Soul*. Who'd have thought that song (*In My Life*) was about here.

The Monument On Ben Bhraggie

Golspie

Atop the hill (pron 'Brachee') that dominates the town, the domineering statue and plinth (over 35m) of the dreaded first Duke of Sutherland; there's a campaign group that would like to see it demolished, but it survives yet. Climb from town fountain on marked path. The hill race go up in 10mins but allow 2hrs return. His private view along the NE coast is superb.

McCaig's Tower or Folly

Oban

Oban's gr landmark built in 1897 by McCaig, a local banker, to give 'work to the unemployed' and as a memorial to his family. It's like a temple or coliseum and time has mellowed whatever incongruous effect it may have had originally. The views of the town and the bay are magnificent and it's easy to get up from several points in town centre.

The Victoria Memorial To Albert

Balmoral

Atop the fir-covered hill behind the house, she raised a monument whose distinctive pyramid shape can be seen peeping over the crest from all over the estate. Desolated by his death, the 'broken-hearted' widow had this memorial built in 1862 and spent so much time here, she became a recluse and the Empire trembled. Path begins at shop on way to Lochnagar distillery, 45mins up. Forget Balmoral, all the longing and love for Scotland can be felt here, the gr estate laid out below.

The Prop Of Ythsie

Nr Aberdeen

35km NW city nr Ellon to W of A92, or pass on the 'Castle Trail' since this monument commemorates one George Gordon of Haddo House nearby, who was prime minister 1852-55 (the good-looking guy in the first portrait you come to in the house). Tower visible from all of rolling Aberdeenshire around and there are reciprocal views should you take the easy but unclear route up. On B999 Aber-Tarves rd (Haddo-Pitmeddon on Castle Trail) and 2km from entrance to house. Take rd for the Ythsie (pron 'icy') farms, car park 100m. Stone circle nearby.

The Monument To Hugh MacDiarmid

Langholm

Brilliant piece of modern sculpture by Jake Harvey rapidly rusting on the hill above Langholm 3km from A7 at beginning of path to the Malcolm obelisk from where there are gr views. MacDiarmid, our national poet, was born in Langholm in 1872 and, though they never liked him much after he left, the monument was commissioned and a cairn beside it raised in 1992. The bare hills surround you. The motifs of the sculpture were used by Scotland's favourite Celtic rock band, Runrig, on the cover of their 1993 album, *Amazing Things*.

Memorial To Norman MacCaig

Nr Lochinver

Foll directions for the remarkable Achin's bookshop which is at the start of the walk to Suilven. Simple memorial of Torridon sandstone to Scotland's gr poet who wrote so much about this landscape he loved: Assynt. Some words writ here to guide us on the way, metaphorically speaking.

Murray Monument

Nr New Galloway

Above A712 rd to Newton Stewart about halfway betw. A fairly austere needle of granite to commemorate a 'shepherd boy', one Alexander Murray, who rose to become a professor of Oriental Languages at Edinburgh University in early 19th century. 10min walk up for fine views of Galloway Hills; pleasant waterfall nearby. Just as he, barefoot ...

Smailholm Tower

Nr Kelso & St Boswells

The classic Border tower; plenty of history and romance and a v nice place to stop, picnic whatever. Good views. Nr main rd B6404 or off smaller B6937 – well signposted. Open Apr-Sept 9.30am-6.30pm. For hrs outwith, 01573 460365. But fine to visit at any time.

Scott Monument

East Princes St, Edinburgh

Apr-Sept Mon-Sat 9am-6pm, Sun 10am-6pm; Oct-Mar, Mon-Sat 9am-3pm, Sun 10am-3pm.

0131 529 4068

Design inspiration for Thunderbird 3. This 1844 Gothic memorial to one of Scotland's best-kent literary sons rises 61.5m above the main drag and provides scope for the vertiginous to come to terms with their affliction. 287 steps mean it's no cakewalk; narrow stairwells weed out claustrophobics too. Those who make it to the top are rewarded with fine views. Underneath, a statue of the mournful Sir Walter gazes across at Jenners.

Hidden Or Lost Valley

Glencoe

The secret glen where the ill-fated Macdonalds hid the cattle they stole and which became (with politics and power struggles) their undoing. A narrow wooded cleft passes betw the imposing and gnarled '3 Sisters' Hills into the huge bowl of Coire Gabhail. The place envelops you in its tragic history. Park on the A82 5km from the VC 300m W of 2 white buildings on either side of the rd. Follow path across the R Coe. Ascend keeping burn to left; 1.5km further up, it's best to ford it. Allow 3hrs.

Under Edinburgh Old Town

The Real Mary King's Close 08702 430160; Mercat Tours 0131 557 6464.

Mary King's Close, a medieval st under the Royal Mile closed in 1753; and the Vaults under South Br, built in the 18thC and sealed up around the start of the 19th. Glimpses of a rather smelly subterranean life way back then. Don't get locked in.

The Yesnaby Stacks

Orkney Mainland

A cliff top viewpoint so wild, so dramatic and, at the edge, so precarious that its supernaturalism verges on the uneasy. Shells of lookout posts from the war echo the melancholy spirit of the place. Nr Skara Brae, it's about 30km from Kirkwall.

The Fairy Glen

Skye

A place so strange, it's hard to believe that it's just a geological phenomenon. Entering Uig from Portree on the A855, take rd on rt marked Balnaknock for 2km and enter an area of extraordinary conical hills which, in certain conditions of light and weather, seems to entirely justify its fairy provenance – what else could explain the incredible 365 of these grassy hillocks?

Clava Cairns

Nr Culloden, Inverness

Curious chambered cairns in a grove of trees nr a river in the middle of 21stC nowhere. This can be seriously Blair Witch.

The Clootie Well

On the road betw Tore on the A9 & Avoch

Spooky spooky place, easily missed, tho' now a marked car park nearby. Hundreds of rags hang on tree branches around the spout of an ancient well. They go way back up the hill and have probably been here for decades. Strange vibrations in this place.

Burn O' Vat

Nr Ballater

V odd glacial curiosity, especially when it's deserted. 8km from Ballater towards Aberd on main A93, take A97 for Huntly for 2km to the Muir of Dinnet nature reserve car park – driving thro' forests of strange spindly birch. Some scrambling to reach the huge 'pot' from which the burn flows to L Kinord.

Crichope Linn

Nr Thornhill

A supernatural sliver of glen inhabited by water spirits (and midges). Take rd for Cample on A76 rd just S of Thornhill. At vill (2km) is a wooden sign; take left for 2km. Discreet sign and gate in bank on rt; quarry for parking 100m further on, on left, is more obvious. Take care – can very slippy. Gorge is a 10-min schlep from the gate.

Sallochy Wood

Loch Lomond

The old hamlet of Wester Sallochy stands surrounded by gloomy conifers, its roofless houses awaiting the return of long-dead tenants. Not a place to visit at night... Marked trail off the B837, N of Balmaha, from Sallochy Wood car park.

Ferry Oban-Craignure, 45mins. Main route; 6 a day. Lochaline-Fishnish, 15mins. 9-15 a day. Kilchoan-Tobermory, 35mins. 7 a day (Sun: summer only). Winter sailings: call TIC.

WHERE TO STAY

Highland Cottage

Tobermory
01688 302030
6RMS MAR-OCT
T/T XPETS CC
KIDS MED.EXP

Breadalbane St opp fire stn. Trad Tobermory st above harbour (from r/bout on rd in from Craignure). Their reputation grows and it's harder to get in but foodies should try. Everything here is small but perfectly formed – relaxed atmos with fine dining.

Tiroran House

Mull
01681 705232
6RMS + 2COTT
JAN-DEC X/T
XPETS CC KIDS
EXP

SW corner on rd to Iona from Craignure then B8035 round Loch na Keal. 1 hr Tobermory. Family-friendly small co house in fabulous gdns by the sea, being refurb under new owners Laurence Mackay & Katie Munro (Katie a Cordon Bleu cook). Excl food from sea & kitchen gdn. Lovely rms. Sea eagles fly over, otters in the bay.

Argyll Hotel

Iona
01681 700334
15RMS FEB-NOV
X/X PETS CC
KIDS MED.INX

On beautiful, turquoise bay betw Iona & Mull on rd betw ferry & abbey. Daytrippers come & go but stay! This is a charming hotel & a remarkable island. Cosy rms (1 suite), good food (esp vegn) fresh from the organic garden. The real peace & quiet – it's Colourist country & this is where they would have stayed too.

Glengorm Castle

Nr Tobermory
01688 302321
5RMS JAN-DEC
X/X PETS CC
KIDS EXP

Minor rd N of town. Glen Gormenghast! Fab views to Ardnamurchan from this baronial pile. Luxurious bedrms in family home – use the library & grand public spaces. Loads of art, lawn & gardens. Excl self-cat cotts on estate. B&B only.

Calgary Farmhouse

Calgary
01688 400256
9RMS MAR-NOV
X/T PETS CC
KIDS MED.INX

7kms S of Dervany nr beautiful Calgary Beach. Roadside bistro/restau with rms and gallery/coffee shop. Island hospitality: Matthew's furniture in public rms & 'Art in Nature' sculpture walking woods at back down to the beach. Get up early to see the otters (I never have). 2 self-cat suites above gallery. Good mod-Brit cooking.

Tobermory Hotel

Tobermory
01688 302091
16RMS JAN-DEC
X/T PETS CC KIDS
MED.INX

On waterfront. Creature comforts, gr outlook in the middle of Balamory bay. 10 rms to front. Restau ok & others nearby.

Ptarmigan House

Tobermory
01688 302863
4RMS MAR-NOV
X/T XPETS
CC XKIDS
MED.INX

Above the town (ask for golf course, it's adj clubhouse) & above all that. Modern, almost purpose-built GH. High-spec rms with gr views and... a swimming pool. Sue & Michael Fink have pushed the boat out since they left the Western Isles (quel demise!). Evening meals on request.

S.Y Hostel

Tobermory
01688 302481

In main st looking out to Tobermory Bay. Central rel high standard hostel v busy in summer. 39 places 7 rms (4 on front). Kitchen. Internet. Nr ferry to Ardnamurchan main Oban ferry 35km away. Mar-Oct. Door 11.45pm.

Caravan Parks

At Fishnish (all facs, nr Ferry) Craignure and Fionnphort:

Camping

Calgary Beach, Fishnish and at Loch Na Keal shore. All fab.

WHERE TO EAT

The Dining Room @ Highland Cottage

Tobermory
01688 302030
MED

Jo Currie's down-to-earth fine dining; destination for foodies, a treat for locals. Impeccably sourced. Nae nonsense! Small so must book.

Dovecote Restaurant

Calgary
01688 400256
INX

7km from Dervaig on B8073 at Calgary Farmhouse. Roadside farm setting for a bistro/wine bar restau using local produce in Mod-Brit cuisine. Gallery/coffee shop in summer. Mellow people, art/sculpture everywhere. A quiet spot for most ambient meal on Mull. Coolest dining rm on the island.

Glengorm Farm Coffee Shop

Nr Tobermory
01688 302321

First right on Tobermory-Dervaig rd. Organic food served in well refurbed stable block. Soups, cakes, venison burgers... all you need after a walk in the grounds of this gr estate & gr ceramics adj. LO 4.30pm. Easter-Oct.

Ulva House

Nr Tobermory
01688 302044

Above town (via Back Brae, past Western Isles Hotel). Excl seafood restau/dining rm, a conservatory-like space with only 16 covers. Spectacular seafood platter. Gr fresh produce & service. Awards in the post, methinks. AYR. Dinner only. Must book.

The Anchorage

Tobermory
01688 302313
INX

Main St opp pier. Best on the bay. Seafood, steaks, specials, good vegn options. Homely & friendly & keen to impress. 7 days, lunch and LO 9pm. Winter hrs vary.

Mull Pottery

Tobermory
01688 302592

Fun mezzanine café above working pottery just outside Tobermory on rd S to Craignure. Evening meals (best atmos) & usual daytime offerings tho' all home-baking. Locals do recommend. AYR. 7 days. LO 9pm.

Meditteranea

Salen
01680 300200
INX

In mid-vill on main Craignure-Tobermory rd. A real, & I mean *real* Italian restau run by Scottish guy & extended Italian family. Mama in kitchen pure Sicilian. So excl pasta, salads, puds & specials with Italian twist. All islands should have one of these. Mar-Oct. Dinner only LO 9pm.

Island Bakery

Tobermory
01688 302225
CHP

Main St. Bakery-deli with excl take-away pizza by Joe Reade, the son of the cheese people. Home-made pâtés, quiches, salads & old-fashioned baking. Buy your picnic here. 7 days LO 7.15pm (w/end only in wint).

The Chip Van aka The Fish Pier

Tobermory
01688 302390
CHP

Tobermory's famous meals-on-wheels underneath the clock tower on the bay. Usual fare but fresh as... and usually a queue. The situation is unquestionably fine. Apr-Dec, noon-9pm. Cl Suns.

Javiers

Tobermory
01688 302365
INX

Far corner of the bay above MacGochan's pub. Argentinian chef, mix-match & Mexican meals. Building local rep at time of going to press. Reports please. AYR. Lunch & LO 9.30pm.

The listing below gives the very best places to stay, eat and drink, where the quality on offer makes them among the best in the UK, rated with two or three ticks. Details of all the places listed, along with many others, can be found in the complete edition of *Scotland the Best*. In each category below, the listing is alphabetical by place.

1 Hotels

Aberdeen *Marcliffe of Pitfodels*

Auchterarder *Gleneagles*

Auldearn nr Nairn *The Boath House*

Ballachulish *Ballachulish House*

Ballantrae nr Girvan *Glenapp Castle*

Ballater *Darroch Learg*

nr Balquidder *Monachyle Mhor*

Banchory *Raemoir House*

Benderloch *Dun na Mara*

Bishopton, nr Glasgow *Mar Hall*

nr Blairgowrie *Kinloch House*

Callander *The Roman Camp*

Crieff *Crieff Hydro*

Crinan *Crinan Hotel*

Dunblane *Cromlix House*

nr Dunkeld *Kinnaird*

Edinburgh, Princes St *The Balmoral*

Edinburgh, 35 Drumsheugh Gardens *The Bonham*

Edinburgh, Princes St *The Caledonian Hilton*

Edinburgh, 34 Gr King St *The Howard*

Edinburgh, Castlehill, Inner Sanctum and Old Rectory *The Witchery*

Edinburgh, Priestfield Rd *Prestonfield*

Edinburgh, North Bridge *The Scotsman*

Edinburgh, Festival Sq, Lothian Rd *The Sheraton Grand*

Fort William *Inverlochy Castle*

Glasgow, 1 Devonshire Gdns *One Devonshire Gardens*

Glasgow, 301 Argyle St *Radisson SAS*

Glasgow, 190 Bath St *St Jude's*

Glen Torridon, nr Kinlochewe *Loch Torridon*

Gullane *Greywalls*

Inverness *Glenmoriston Townhouse*

Linlithgow *Champany Inn*

Loch Awe *Ardanaiseig*
Lochinver *The Albannach*
nr Oban *Isle of Eriska*
Poolewe *Pool House Hotel*
Port Appin *Airds Hotel*
Portpatrick *Knockinaam Lodge*
Skibo Castle, Dornoch *The Carnegie Club*
Colbost, Skye *The House Over-by*
South Shore Loch Tay *Ardeonaig*
St Andrews *Old Course*
Turnberry *The Westin Turnberry Resort*
Ullapool *The Ceildh Place*
nr Wick *Ackergill Tower*

2 Restaurants

Aberdeen *Silver Darling*
Anstruther *The Cellar*
Auchterader *Andrew Fairlie at Gleneagles*
Auldean, nr Nairn *The Boath House*
Bridgend of Lintrathen *Lochside Lodge*
Colbost, Skye *The Three Chimneys*
Crossmichael, nr Castle Douglas *The Plumed Horse*
nr Cupar *The Peat Inn*
Edinburgh, 14 Bonnington Rd *Big Fish*
Edinburgh, 3 Hunter Sq *Creelers*
Edinburgh, St Mary's St *David Banns*
Edinburgh, 49 Thistle St *Dusit*
Edinburgh, The Shore, Leith *Fishers*
Edinburgh, 58 Thistle St *Fishers in the City*
Edinburgh, 96 Dalry Rd *La Partenhope*
Edinburgh, 54 The Shore, Leith *Martin Wishart*
Edinburgh, 1a Dock Pl, Leith *Skippers*
Edinburgh, Castlehill *The Witchery*
Glasgow, 89 Candleriggs *Dahkin*
Glasgow, Glass House, Springfield Court *Etain*
Glasgow, 225a W George St *Gamba*
Glasgow, 28 Westminster Terr *Mother India*
Gullane *La Potinière*
Inverness *Abstract @ The Glenmoriston*
Perth *63 Tay Street*

Perth *Let's Eat*
Scrabster *The Captain's Galley*
St Andrews *The Seafood Restaurant*
St Monans *The Seafood Restaurant*
Troon *MacCallum's of Troon Oyster Bar*

3 Tearooms, Coffee Shops & Cafés

Aboyne *The Black-Faced Sheep*
Banchory *Falls of Freugh*
Edinburgh, Belford Rd *Gallery (of Modern Art) Café*
Edinburgh, 257 Canongate *Plaisir du Chocolat*
Edinburgh, National Portrait Gallery, Queen St *Queen Street Café*
Edinburgh, Brunswick St *Vittoria*
Glasgow, 64 Albion St *Café Gandolfi*
Glasgow, 87 Byres Rd *University Café*
Inverness *The Castle Restaurant*
nr Kinross *The Powmill Milkbar*
Tibbermore, nr Perth *Gloagburn Farm and Coffeeshop*
Tyndrum *Green Welly Stop*
Tyndrum *Real Food Café*

4 Pubs & Gastropubs

Achiltibuie *Summer Isles Hotel Bar*
Edinburgh, 237 Morningside Rd *The Canny Man*
Edinburgh, West Port *Dragonfly*
Edinburgh, 36 The Shore, Leith *King's Wark*
Edinburgh, 233 Causewayside *The New Bell*
Edinburgh, 58 Constitution St *Port O'Leith*
Edinburgh, 3 The Shore, Leith *The Shore*
Glasgow, 64 Albion St *Bar Gandolfi*
Glasgow, 266 Bath St *The Griffin*
Glasgow, 17 Drury St *The Horseshoe*
Glasgow, 28-30 Gibson St *Stravaigin*
Inverarnan, nr Ardlui *The Drover's Inn*
Kippen *The Inn at Kippen*
Lauder *The Black Bull*
Sorn, nr Mauchline *Sorn Inn*
St Andrews *Grange Inn*
Tobermory *The Mishnish*